Random Ambiguity Generational Mental Illness and Me

By Joel Sissel

Copyright 2026 ISBN #979-8-234-17852-7

"Dedicated to my family who taught me how to live again. And to Patrick, Joe, and the countless others who didn't make it--you are never left behind."

Forward

"There is a kind of sadness that comes from knowing too much, from seeing the world as it truly is. It is the sadness of understanding that life is not a grand adventure, but a series of small insignificant moments, that love is not a fairy tale but a fragile, fleeting emotion, that happiness is not a permanent state, but a rare, fleeting glimpse of something we can never hold onto. And in that understanding, there is a profound loneliness, a sense of being cut off from the world, from other people, from oneself."

-Virginia Woolf

The Haunting

"the only way out is through."

-Robert Frost

I really do not want to go to Patrick's memorial service. I've never been a big fan of death ceremonies. In fact, I've only been to five or six in my entire lifetime. That's a pretty good record considering how old I am. But this ceremony, this celebration of life is going to be especially difficult for me for many reasons. I've been dreading going for weeks. Maybe, maybe I could pretend to be sick. I know that sounds selfish, but the circumstances of Patrick's death are a little too close to the bone for my taste. His death was a terrible shock to everyone, a horrible tragedy. When I heard about it, it literally sucked the air from my lungs like a heavy punch to the gut.

Patrick and I were not really close. He was my wife's younger cousin and we would sometimes see each other on holidays and at family get-togethers. When we did see each other, we would usually have deep conversations about the state of the world and education as we saw it. One of my favorite memories of Patrick was the time we shared a little too much Jameson Whiskey on St. Patrick's Day. Patrick was of course Irish.

Even though we had only seen each other a handful of times, Patrick and I were very much alike in many ways. Patrick was a musician, so am I. He got into teaching relatively late in life, like me, and he was a middle school social studies teacher, just like I was. He was a kind soul, someone you felt like you'd known from the moment you met. It was easy to feel a connection with Patrick and I considered him to be a good friend.

As a teacher, Patrick was known for his tea drinking, but more importantly, for his ability to connect with students and challenge them with real-life questions. His students adored him. In 2025 he was awarded the prestigious WHO 13 Golden Apple Award for teaching excellence. Just months later he would be dead. We lived parallel lives Patrick and I, even though he was 20 years younger.

No, I think I'll stay home from Patrick's memorial. I think that would be for the best. I'd have to face some very harsh realities if I went. I'd have to answer some tough questions that I've been avoiding. Dammit! I have to go—my wife's entire family will be there, but most importantly, my son will be there.

I think that life is the art of distraction. To enjoy life and to have what most people would consider a successful and happy existence, one must master the art of distraction. Distractions shield us from realizing the true nature and horrors of life, our short and rather insignificant existence, and the fragility of the things we take for granted. Distractions help us not get too bogged down with things like war, poverty, cruelty, inhumanity, starvation, disease, loss, death, and all the other harsh realities we avoid. Distractions keep us from thinking too much. Distractions—such as love, sex, music, family, work, food, television, literature—you name it—if it's not awful and ugly, it's a distraction. Yup! Life is the art of distraction. The better you are at it, the happier you'll be.

I've lost the art of distraction.

My family has had its fair share of run-ins with mental illnesses. Anorexia, obsessive compulsive disorder, depression, mania, and last but not least severe anxiety. That's just my immediate family, I don't know much about our past generations, but my gut tells me it was there too. What I can tell you is that growing up in my family involved a heavy dose of sarcasm and cynicism with a sense of humor to match. We looked at the world a little differently. We were a cynical bunch with a wicked sense of observation. It was and still is a severely judgmental microscope of ourselves and others, with a deep, often unhealthy humility and insecurity. Internal and external self-awareness on steroids. The real world often seemed foreign, sometimes ridiculous, and out of our reach. We didn't seem to fit in, in other words. At least that's how I felt. I guess I thought our family was special, in a good way, and I was glad that I seemed to think differently than just about anybody else that I met.

As I grew older most of my family members were diagnosed with mental illnesses. For some, these illnesses went painfully undiagnosed for many years. Eventually, all but my oldest sister Jenna and I were treated with various medicines, treatments and hospitalizations for their own unique mental illnesses. But I guess I thought I was different. I told myself I would never ever become depressed or manic like my father. I swore I would never fall victim to crippling anxiety like my mother. I promised myself I would never become obsessive compulsive like my sister Andrea. I was strong. I could fight it off.

I had a good run, I made it into my fifties, but as I examined my past, it became quite obvious that I had shown signs of mental illness throughout the various stages of my life. I had indeed inherited the generational mental illnesses that occupied our family, both past and present. The signs were there all along. Frankly, it was a bit absurd and brash for me to think I could remain ignorant and immune. I somehow believed I would make it through this life unscathed from the mental health gene pool of my family. I guess when you're in the thick of it, you can't see the forest for the trees, or the illness from the normal—until one day it blows a hole in your head.

It's very likely that my dad committed suicide at the ripe old age of 73. My middle sister, Andrea, and I have our suspicions, and it wouldn't surprise us in the least. My oldest sister, Jenna, might have a hard time believing it to be true. But Andrea and I both find it highly probable that he did. I think my mother may have considered it a possibility as well. However, it was only brought up once between the four of us during the grieving family services. He died "in his sleep," as they say. We didn't think it was something to pursue with an autopsy.

For some reason, it does not bother me in the least that my dad may have taken his own life. It probably should, but it doesn't. He was that kind of person. Brutally honest… unflinchingly honest. Honest enough to know when he'd had enough, and strong enough to look death (or God) in the eye and say, "I'll be leaving now."

He suffered from various things: depression, mania, neuropathy of the feet, high intellect, deep thinking, and a realistic grasp of his own existence. But mainly, he suffered. Long and deep. Much like me and my middle sister. We're a couple of chips off the old block, as my dad would say.

"There is only one serious philosophical question, and that is 'suicide.' This, according to Albert Camus. His philosophy of the absurd summed up human fate: Sisyphus endlessly pushing his rock up the mountain only to see it roll back down each time he got near the top. Those Greeks sure knew how to punish someone. But they were also astute at grasping the absurdity of life. I must admit that I often feel like Sisyphus. Life is hard. Really hard. And scary if you allow yourself to think about it too much. If you ask me, it is one serious leap of faith to step out into this world and live.

To be sure, I'm lucky to be here at all. I honestly don't know how I made it this far. I really shouldn't be here. The fact that I am here almost makes me believe in miracles—or possibly curses? I mean, really, I should be on the streets, in the grave, or somewhere else far less fortunate. The odds were not good, from where I sit looking back on my life. The things I did seem very risky to me now, yet here I am—somehow, miraculously, here. Dumb luck in my case. Let's just say I had a lot of help. I mean, a lot of help. Everybody needs help. Some more than others.

Let's just clear things up right off the bat. Trying to define or describe anxiety disorder and depression from an experiential point of view is nearly impossible. Anyone who has ever experienced either one will tell you that you really can't know what it's like unless you've experienced it yourself. If you have experienced these things, you will most likely relate to some of what is shared here. If you haven't experienced them but know someone who has, then maybe this book will help you understand a fraction of what their life is like.

Realistically, most people don't want to be bothered with such things as depression and anxiety. They are not wired for such thoughts and feelings and cannot, in their wildest imagination, fathom such "weakness" or loss of control. They think depression and anxiety are not really diseases but flaws in a person's effort or will. "Suck it up and deal", "Get over it" in other words. Other people, I think, live their lives on a wire, tittering on fragility and loss of control, so much so that they dare not even think about things that would cause anxiety or depression for fear of falling off that wire. They occupy themselves with religion, money, power, greed, sex, and any number of things that keep their minds off thinking too much.

Distraction… in other words.

Let's see what the experts say, shall we?

The Mayo Clinic attempts to define anxiety disorder as "intense, excessive, and persistent worry and fear about everyday situations." Often, anxiety disorders involve repeated episodes of sudden feelings of intense anxiety and fear, or terror, that reach a peak within minutes (panic attacks). Depression is a mood disorder that causes a persistent feeling of sadness and loss of interest. It affects how you feel, think, and behave, and can lead to a variety of emotional and physical problems. That's the best clinical definition I could find for anxiety disorder and depression, but they do not come remotely close to the actual experience.

Here's what I know about anxiety disorder. It never gives up. You might as well get used to it being your lifelong companion. It will be with you until the end of your days. Once it has it's hooks in you, it does not let go. There is no cure. There is no magic drug. There is no magic therapy. Anxiety just becomes a part of you. It weaves its way into the fabric of who you are and becomes embedded within your very makeup. In my case, the roots of severe anxiety are a propensity that has been passed down and inherited from the genes of past generations—a deadly gene that lies dormant, waiting. Waiting for the perfect conditions and the perfect storm. Waiting for the fire to be lit.

There doesn't have to be a specific cause for anxiety disorder, although I am quite sure of the causes of mine—or should I say, the igniting circumstances. Anxiety has a life of its own, and it comes and goes whenever it damn well pleases. It's as though a switch has been turned on in you that can never be turned off. This switch makes everything, every situation, every event, every chore, every relationship—intensified to the point of breakdown. You no longer see everyday activities as casual, run-of-the-mill experiences. Nor do you go about your day in any normal sense of the word.

Nope—your world is hyper-awareness. Each activity feels like the end of the world. Every minute before an event is agonized over. Every difficult situation involving relationships is life changing. It is being completely and utterly overwhelmed. Just living is lost. Let me repeat that: just living is lost. Even the simplest things—getting dressed, deciding what to eat, taking a shower, doing something you once enjoyed—are lost.

The switch scrambles the puzzle pieces of you that were once put together and functioning, mixing them up so that they no longer fit. Severe anxiety is the loss of hope, but more importantly, it is the loss of two things that all humans must have and take for granted. The first is the simple belief, or unconscious knowing, that everything will somehow be alright. The second is the ability to forgive yourself. Things will not be alright when you have severe anxiety, and you will definitely not be forgiven.

You try to live and go about your day, but it takes superhuman effort to keep anxiety at bay. Feelings of fear, inadequacy, imperfection, self-awareness, and worry haunt you every minute of every day. It is a fight you will most likely lose several times a day, yet still, you must keep fighting—scratching and clawing, tooth and nail—to keep your world from completely unraveling and falling apart.

Anxiety comes in different strengths and varieties, and it likes to partner up with its good friend, depression. Depression is well established in my family's past, mostly on my father's side, and has often been something I have battled with throughout my adult life—though I never knew it until recent self-examination and the writing of this book.

For me, anxiety makes it almost impossible to start any task, for fear of a million different reasons, while depression takes away any excitement or energy needed to undertake the task and ultimately makes every task meaningless. *What's the point, in other words? Nothing matters.*

Sometimes anxiety simply gives me a subtle nudge or twinge, just to say, "Hello there." Other times, it feels like my whole world is caving in and the only way to survive is to take a pill. Once in a while, anxiety will leave me alone for an hour or two, and I can almost feel like myself again. But beware—don't get too comfortable. Just when I think I've reached a safe distance, anxiety taps me on the shoulder and says, "I'm still here." Then it slaps me in the face, punches me in the gut, throws me to the ground, and stomps all over me, laughing all the while at my foolish belief that I was free.

Most times, anxiety is just there—keeping me from relaxing, preventing me from simply being, preventing me from being present. It does not allow me to live in the moment or to enjoy anything, because I am always looking to the future. The future of what, though? I am aware of anxiety's presence constantly. It is a bit like being haunted—like the frightening books I've read and the scary movies I've watched. Anxiety is the ghost tormentor who will never release me—the ghost of past, present, and future all rolled into one complete package of torture.

Oh, to simply be. To be free from the haunting and the fear. What a wonderful thing that would be. How I miss that feeling—or non-feeling. How I wish I could just go about my day without this constant awareness.

Anxiety is merciless and without remorse, and quite happy to have me as its close friend. It frolics in my misery and enjoys my company. Often, after a severe attack, I must begin again at ground zero, rebuilding my fragile existence to hopefully withstand the next onslaught. It is torture, followed by a brief respite. My only relief is sleep, with the help of medication—a few hours of nothing, if I'm lucky. But mean old anxiety is there when I wake up.

"Good morning," it says as I open my eyes. "What shall we do today?"

"Survive motherfucker," I say, *"just survive!"*

It's not like I woke up one morning and discovered that I was no longer myself. I did not just become broken in one day, even though it seemed that way at the time. No—it took years of unimaginable pressure and stress. Years of self-awareness and self-critical behavior. Years of insulating myself from feeling too much emotion and keeping everything under perceived, manageable control, brewing, fermenting, festering, and stewing in my own self-contained hell.

It all seemed so normal. And on top of it all was the kick-start from the gene pool I inherited—from my mother and father, and their parents before them. What seemed normal exploded into a full-blown, out-of-control disaster.

As the song goes, "All the things we could never see—one day, they will blow a hole in our heads." Lyrics my old friend Charles, the lead singer of my band 23 Lies, wrote—words that have stayed with me to this day. There's a hole in my head, and I am broken. I am definitely broken.

I'm hanging on. Sometimes by a thread. It has become increasingly evident that I probably am not going to make it—day to day, hour to hour. Anxiety, panic, and fear are my daily companions. I have reached moments where I cannot take it anymore. I just can't go on.

What do I do? I take a Lorazepam and hope for the best. Most times, it works for a while and calms me enough to survive. Let's face it—life has never come easy for me, but I've never experienced anything like this before.

Some moments are so unbearable that the only relief feels like it would be to end it somehow. "Make it stop," I plead to something—anything—"Please, make it stop." But there is no answer. I sob, I cry, I drop to my knees. Thankfully, after a few intense minutes that feel like hours, it subsides—like being violently sick after too much to drink or a bout with the flu. The heaving finally ends, leaving me quivering and wrung out on the floor.

Nothing comes naturally to me, and it never really has. The more I look back on my past, the more I can see the seeds of anxiety and depression. They were there all along—in my childhood, in my aloneness and abnormal self-awareness; in my teenage years, in aloofness, detachment, and fantasy; in my young adulthood, in failure, drugs, and relationships; in adulthood, in depression, songwriting, and the constant need to reinvent myself.

Finally, those seeds took root in the perfect environment: parenthood, teaching, trauma, stress, and the crippling awareness of a life that had peaked and was now declining. Only now can I look back and recognize the times I was manic and the times I was depressed. It seems obvious now—but then, it was normal, and I could survive and move on.

These days, I often find myself detached from my body, watching myself from above in a state of anxiety hell. But I fight through it and come back to myself—partially, somehow, some way. I try not to rely on Lorazepam, but lately I think it might be best to return to it full-time.

I've gotten a little better since retiring from teaching. The frequency of anxiety attacks has lessened. Only now and then do I end up curled in a ball on the floor—a shaking, horrified mess. I don't often wake up soaked in sweat in the middle of the night from panic attacks. I still experience body spasms, but not every day.

My anxiety is still constant, still crippling, but it is no longer about which students will traumatize me today. Now it's about money, my relationships with my wife and son, their health, aging, unfulfilled dreams, daily responsibilities, the state of the world—or nothing at all but uncertainty and fear. Always fear.

The world is just too big when you have severe anxiety. It feels as if everything is fragile—not just in my life, but in everyone and everything around me.

Random and Ambiguous

"Neurosis is the inability to tolerate ambiguity."
-Sigmund Freud

The word *random* is defined as "determined by accident rather than design." *Ambiguous* is defined as "capable of being understood in two or more possible ways." The title and subject of this book relate to what I perceive as the random and ambiguous nature of life—my life specifically, examined through the lens of someone who thinks too much and, for some reason, demands an explanation for this randomness and ambiguity. I do not tolerate ambiguity well at all.

You see, I believe that the life we have created for ourselves is not exactly a divine plan, but rather more like an intentional accident, much of it a result of chance and happenstance. Sure, some of it was planned and shaped by personal effort, but ultimately it is just random, ambiguous interactions: attempts, failures, successes, changes, and meetings with people. I'm sure everyone can look back on their lives and see crucial events or encounters that altered their course.

I've reached a stage in my life where I seriously question whether there is any real purpose behind what feels like randomness. Sometimes I get a fleeting desire to run for my life. But I'm too entrenched—and too weak—to claw my way out anyway. Besides, where would I go? What would I do? Years of digging my own hole—life, my grave, have left me with four steep walls surrounding me. There is no ladder.

Yet, I keep digging because it's easier than figuring out how to build one. It's a very nice place to be, especially for a grave. Comfortable, loving, and, in its own way, great. But it gnaws at me that the outcome of my life has been completely random and ambiguous: full of accidental encounters with people, influences, and circumstances; made up of ambiguous choices, opportunities, and decisions. All this leads me to the conclusion that nothing really matters. Nothing at all. Everything makes a difference—and yet nothing matters. I could have encountered an infinite number of different circumstances, people, and stimuli and become someone completely different. I could have made other choices along the way, and my life would be entirely different. And yet, it still wouldn't matter. I would still be me, right?

I have often asked myself: If I weren't me, who would I be? Would I exist at all? If one of my parents had been different, would I still be me. Like partially me—or someone completely different? I began asking these questions as a little boy, but never out loud, only to myself. From the very beginning, I suppose I was an existentialist. I even had to look up the definition to be sure I was using the word correctly. Existentialism: "the philosophical belief that we are each responsible for creating purpose in our own lives." Doomed, in other words.

As I grew older, the questions evolved. Did I exist before this current form in an unconscious state, just waiting for the opportunity to present itself—a soul in waiting? Am I an evolving self, changing with each new version of life? Do I exist in the non-physical world, moving from this body to another, or did the universe somehow conspire to create… me? The "me" that will exist for a relatively short period, as the one and only me, never to exist again. Could it really be that simple? Am I just a product of random circumstance—the collision of my parents in an infinite world of possibilities? Is that really it?

My father had a pocket Bible, passed down from his father, and his father before him, which he in turn gave to me. My great grandfather kept this Bible in his breast pocket during the Civil War. It bears the indentation of a musket ball in the lower right corner. The inscription reads: *"Battle of Champions Hill, Miss., May 16, 1863. This book hit with a musket ball here."* In other words, this book saved my great grandfather's life. Had it not been in his pocket, the entire history of my family might have been very different—or not exist at all. If that isn't random ambiguity, I don't know what is.

You might be thinking, "Who cares about this? Why bother with such questions?" Well, I do, I care greatly. I struggle with these questions because, surely it cannot be pure accident that we are who we are—and yet, surely it could be. This paradox leaves me feeling profoundly, exquisitely ambiguous.

Etm (I'm not telling you, look it up.)

I wish it would rain. Somehow, I would feel better if it just rained. Rainy days have a way of removing guilt. They allow you to dote about, do nothing, or very little— without feeling bad about it. A thunderstorm would be even better. I have always loved storms, the more frequent the lightning and the louder the thunder, the better. To me, storms relieve the burden of thinking. They allow me, rarely, to just live in the moment and realize how small I am —and how powerful Mother Nature is.

I would like to know what it is like to be you. To climb inside your head and swim around a bit. Then I might know if I am truly alone. I might know whether these things that I think about are abnormal or in some way unusual. It would give me great comfort to know that someone else felt and thought about the world in a similar way. Some of my greatest joys in life come from finding kinship with others. Connecting in some small way. To share the same experiences, doubts, thoughts, and feelings. This has always been hard for me to find, and even harder as I get older. I have felt kinship through art, such as songwriters, writers, and artists. Songs, books, and paintings that tell me I am not alone in this world. I am an observer, for sure, and I am always curious about people. What are their lives really like? Are they happy? What do they think about? How do they feel? I'd like to believe that other people's lives look better, happier, and more interesting than they really and truly are. You know, "they look so happy, God, I hope they have some hidden, dark, and awful thing they suffer from." That's what I tell myself sometimes to make myself feel better about my life.

"Comparisons are odious," someone once said. I don't know who, but I agree. They stink in every way. Comparing yourself to others is never good for you. It doesn't matter if you fare far better or worse, in the comparison, they nevertheless still reek of foulness, rot, and decay, because comparing implies that your life isn't good enough for you. Still, I find myself comparing my life to others quite often. Everything is relative though. Everyone has regrets, desires, fantasies, sorrows, needs, and dreams, etc. There are just different degrees and intensities, and most importantly, differences in how one interprets and processes all of them. Everyone shits, to put it bluntly. Everyone is a nobody, and everybody is somebody. Every person has a story to tell that is full of drama, suffering, joy, sadness, love, passion, regret, desire, loss, and other things too numerous to list. Don't they? I think there is a novel in everyone. Some just choose to write it down.

I've often wondered about the real lives of actors and actresses. Those truly talented ones who are able to portray characters so convincingly that you believe that they are who they pretend to be. Their ability to become almost anyone makes me wonder how they keep their true selves together. If I were an actor, I think it would be difficult for me not to take on characteristics of those characters whom I portray and lose a part of myself with every role. I also think it would be somewhat hard to discern between reality and fantasy, having to go in and out of each so often and so thoroughly that the lines would become somewhat blurred. Portraying someone falling in love would be exciting and confusing, just as it is in real life, only how could you not keep yourself from feeling attraction, some true emotions and love for some of your co-stars. In other words, to some degree, acting might actually become reality and vice versa. Playing different roles in make-believe worlds, living many different lives, and spending a good portion of your life in fantasy. Not to mention getting paid quite a bit for doing so. Like recess to an emotional playground. Wait a minute, I actually do spend much of my time in fantasy, but I don't receive money for it, instead, I receive awkwardness, isolation, and longing. I naively think being an actor would be the life for me. I could leave each fantasy at the end and then cleanly move on to another one. But, we are all actors, though, aren't we? Taking on the roles of father, husband, artist, friend, lover, teacher. Playing our part, taking on characteristics of some of the people we meet and admire along the roads of our lives. We are sponges and absorbers, mixing what we take in with what we already have and baking it all up into what we are becoming. Always becoming.

But, I digress. You do know the title of this book is *Random Ambiguity*, right? It is fitting not only for the content, but also for the writing style. So, you knew what you were getting into when you picked it up. No apologies necessary, I hope.

Our Story Begins

"There is no such thing as a happy ending. I never met a single one to equal Once Upon a Time."
-Stephen King

Once upon a time (No tale would be complete without this.), I was telling a friend about some of my more adventurous experiences. This person told me, "you should write a book." I was in much better shape mentally at that time, younger, etc., but it stuck with me. I have no idea how to write a book. My father wrote a book. It wasn't published, and to be honest, I'm sorry to say that I didn't really enjoy it that much. I'm not sure my attempt will be any more interesting or successful, but I thought I would give it a whirl. Besides, I'm not really writing this for the benefit of the reader; I'm doing it selfishly for me. I think of it as a purge, therapy, something cathartic, or even an indulgence. It is an attempt to make sense of the suffering and to understand my history and my family's history of mental health. It is a book written in the style of the title and my life. It is a journal, if you will, of my journey through life, both past and present, through recklessness, craziness, inherited anxiety and depression, near-death experiences, and last but not least, getting old. To be honest, I'm not sure I'm going to make it through the anxiety and depression or the getting old parts. Right now, none of it is going well.

I often look at people and say to myself, "Is life supposed to be easy?" It sure looks to me like some people make living look easy. Does living just come naturally for some people? Do they just simply live with confidence and surety about their purpose and the choices they have made? Did they plan their life and end up with exactly what they wanted life to be? Do they go about the business of living without deeply thinking about their own existence, without self-awareness, as if on a line from start to finish? Do they think too much like me? Do they have doubts? Do they have this inner voice that I have?

I sometimes ask myself, how did I get here? How did I arrive at this place, with these people and these things? What happened to my dreams? What were my dreams? Is this life my dreams fulfilled? What did I want to be, who did I want to be? You forget your life after a while. The life you knew at one time gives way to another, and then another. What you thought and hoped and wished your life to be gets lost in living, like beads on a necklace, broken and scattered on the floor. Lost in dark places, rarely, if ever, to be seen again. You pick up the ones that you find and make a new necklace, only to have it break again. And so on.... Pretty soon the necklace is nothing but a few beads on a string that no longer make a necklace, but a keepsake in the drawer. You always try to move forward, move on with your life, making the best of what you have. Sometimes you try to remember what those lost beads looked like and where they could possibly have disappeared to. Once in a while, you find one. It vaguely looks familiar, but it's too much work to put it back on the string to make a new necklace. It might bring a smile to your face or a wince, or even make you cry for what was and what will never be again. But you cast it aside, put it in the drawer with the rest of the other beads; sometimes you even throw it away. Like those dreams you once had.

Forks in the Road

“Alice came to a fork in the road. ‘Which road do I take?’ She asked. ‘Where do you want to go?’ responded the Cheshire Cat. ‘I don’t know,’ Alice answered. ‘Then,’ said the Cat, ‘it doesn’t matter.”

-Lewis Carroll

Someone once asked the Irish playwright George Bernard Shaw what he thought the most beautiful thing in the world was. “Youth,” he replied. “Youth is the most beautiful thing in the world, and what a pity that it has to be wasted on children.” What a great line and I agree wholeheartedly, especially from the perspective of an aging man. I have thought about my youth a great deal as of late and wondered about the choices that I made, fate and the thoughts that I had during those days long gone. I have come to the realization that I knew very little about what I was doing. I was the proverbial chicken running around with its head cut off, just bumping into things. I flew by the seat of my pants, seeking as many experiences as I could and learning by trial and error. There was never really a goal or a plan when I was young. I just tried to be honest with myself and others and to live with integrity and passion. But, in reality, I had no idea what the bloody hell I was doing. I don’t think at the time I was aware that I didn’t have a clue. I was really just seeking adventure. Perhaps I was a little too greedy in my search for adventure and youthful desires. I was the boy who refused to grow up. It was a “beautiful” thing.

This brings me to another question. Is it possible that in our lives we are given choices or forks in the road that determine what we will become? Are these forks random and ambiguous, or are they under some divine design? If I took another road would I end up right where I am today? Is it possible that there is a right choice and a wrong one? Would I have been more content and happier taking one road over the other? What would have happened had I taken the other roads? Ambiguity be damned!

I can look back at my life and identify some of these forks, but not all of them. Life does throw you some signs along the way, if you happen to be paying attention. You usually notice them long after they have presented themselves. You say to yourself, “Ah yes, now I see.” I guess some people probably never give these signs another thought. Oh, but I do. It’s not that I have great regret for any of the roads I took or didn’t take. I’m just looking for a little clarity, that’s all, and maybe some historical relevance to my current condition.

One of the first and easiest forks for me to identify was the choice not to become a lawyer. I had studied political science and philosophy at the University of Iowa and considered becoming a lawyer, but thought otherwise after graduating. I then studied to become a paralegal and very much-loved research and writing. I was told by my professors that I was very good at it (I thought so as well) and should consider going to law school. It would have been a natural transition. Not only did I not become a lawyer, but I never became a paralegal either. I found a job instead at an insurance company, which I learned to hate very much. But I also became a singer, songwriter, and rock-and-roll guitarist. Hmmm. Lawyer or rock-and-roll guitarist? A tough choice for anyone, no doubt. For some reason, it never occurred to me that I could do both.

There were other signs and forks throughout my life, some involved music, some women, some geography. There were obvious forks that I took voluntarily and some that were circumstantial, like marrying my first wife. Some signs were probably there but I didn't recognize them then, or even now. All of these forks in the road have contributed greatly to my current existence. But honestly, there was no plan. Remember spinning the globe when you were a kid and stopping it with your finger, claiming, "That's where I will live someday?" Such was my life, a constantly spinning globe.

An Adventurer

"Of all the things I am not very good at, living in the real world is perhaps the most outstanding."
-Bill Bryson

I despise responsibility. I never wanted to become an adult, and fought it off for as long as I possibly could. I even thought about titling this book "The Boy Who Refused to Grow Up." Adulthood has me now though; it has me good, right by the proverbial testicles. I may have mistakenly thought that life was supposed to be exciting and adventurous and meaningful all the time. (Could this be mania?) I may have had unrealistic expectations from reading books and watching television as a young boy running wild in the neighborhood as if I were Tarzan or Zorro or Odysseus. As a young child I once packed some food and clothing in a red bandana, attached to a broom-stick, and attempted to run away from home. Just like the hobo I'd seen on TV. Why did I choose a hobo as a role model at such an early age? I didn't get very far. I got scared.

Later, I sought to emulate my heroes in books by finding adventure on the road or in the wilderness like Kerouac, or the books of Hemingway, or any number of idols of mine. I glorified and over-dramatized life. Perhaps not such a horrible thing to do, but definitely hard to live up to and maintain for an entire life. I never wanted a "normal" life—marriage, a house, a steady job, a couple of kids, etc. What is normal anyway? What was it that made me seek adventure? From my early childhood I felt that life had to have meaning and be lived to its fullest. This to me meant adventure, whether it was riding my bike to places unknown, climbing trees, exploring the woods, or running away from home.

I wanted to travel the world. I wanted to sail around the world. I wanted to climb mountains. I wanted to see the Amazon, Africa, Egypt, everything. My parents bought me a set of children's encyclopedias when I was young. I used to sit for hours reading and looking through those books, dreaming of all the things I could see and do. Eventually however, I was forced to grow up, earn a paycheck and figure out what I wanted to do for a living. This meant first, finding a course of study in college.

I was consumed by music in my teenage years, obsessed with learning to play the guitar at the age of 13. I would spend hours listening to music and learning how to play songs and guitar solos. Secretly, I wanted to be a song writer and rock and roll star. Music was my strongest interest, so I went to college and studied music, playing in rock-and-roll bands on the side. Eventually my major in music was begrudgingly surrendered into merely getting a college degree. I ended up with a political science degree with a minor in philosophy, a practical degree to be sure, and very useful in everyday life.

After college I struggled to find my place in this world. I wrestled with the questions: Where do I belong? What can I do that has meaning, and still make a decent living? My life of adventure had to give way to being somewhat responsible. I still played music in bands and began to write my own songs, but I couldn't reconcile the responsible part of life with the need to have meaning in what I did for a living. Some people are content with doing a job well and don't need to have their work be meaningful. I've had conversations with friends about their work, and most of them don't feel the same way I do. Needless to say, finding a job that fit was difficult, and it took me a long time to figure this conundrum out.

I had several jobs that paid well enough, but they left me feeling empty and purposeless. It wasn't until my thirties that I found teaching, a profession that had meaning to me. Existentialism is a difficult path; life would be so much easier without it. I would definitely be happier if I didn't try to find meaning in all of this mess. The hard truth is that I do search for some meaning and truth. I have gotten lost in this attempt through various endeavors, only to find myself back at my original questions, along with a few more. I had more certainty and more conviction when I was younger, even though I may have been wrong. Now it is a half-hearted effort with much less energy and exuberance and a hell of a lot more distractions.

Sometimes I wish and hope that I (we) get another chance at life after death. I childishly envision a choice at those "pearly gates." The gatekeeper asking the dead as they come to the entrance of heaven, "What would you like to do? Enter the kingdom of heaven and eternal bliss, or… take your chances and roll the dice on another shot at life?" My answer would be, "Roll the dice at life." I don't want to go to heaven and be joyous and serene and at one with the universe, or whatever heaven might or might not be. (However, as I get older, joy and serenity sound better and better.) I want to come back and give life another try. I want to suffer and love and experience everything again, but differently. More importantly, I would like another try because I feel as if I didn't quite get this one, this life.

"A New Life Please" is the title of a song I wrote a long time ago. It was written from the perspective of someone who feels damaged and torn to the point of being utterly unusable. I was completely overwhelmed with life. Even as a young man I felt that I was not cut out for this thing called life. I didn't have the skin for it. Too soft, too weak, and too vulnerable. The song was written in my youth, a youth full of thoughts and feelings that I have forgotten or lost, like those beads in the dark corners of places unknown.

Don't misunderstand, my life is not terrible. In fact, it is beautiful! I am fortunate beyond belief with a loving family, reasonably good health, a beautiful home, plenty of food to eat, and lots of distractions. I don't want for anything, really. I am not dissatisfied with the people whom I love and who love me. I am dissatisfied with myself, and myself only.

The Curse

"Life is a tragedy for those who feel, and a comedy for those who think."
-La Bruyere

So, I have to ask: what the hell is life for someone who both thinks and feels too much, to the point of excessive self-awareness and, sometimes, paralysis?

I'm pretty sure I know the answer. It's looking at me in the mirror.

I think too much. I always have. Bad genes, I guess. Very bad genes. It's both a blessing and a curse, but mostly a curse.

As a child, I spent most of my days alone, creating fantasy worlds, talking to no one but myself, silently, in my head. I lived there quite happily, thank you very much, occupying myself by riding my bike, exploring, climbing trees, reading, listening to music, and watching television on a black-and-white TV with only three channels to choose from.

My fantasies came from what I saw on television or read in books. I could also interact with others when needed. I did play sports and sometimes rode bikes with other kids, but I never had a good friend or a best friend. We moved a lot — five times before I turned twelve, so I didn't make any long-lasting friendships. I learned to be self-sufficient, to be alone.

It was a gift, I think, knowing how to be alone. It never bothered me much. In fact, I liked it, and still do. It was a safe place to be, cocooned in my thoughts. We had a pretty good relationship, me and my mind. Or so I thought.

When I was twelve, we moved to Des Moines, Iowa, and I took up the guitar. I spent all my free time listening to music and learning how to play, creating a world of rock-and-roll dreams. Middle school…..ugh. I didn't really make any real friends there either. I just survived and played guitar.

When I was around eighteen years old, I remember distinctly an incident with my family that laid bare my excessive thinking and revealed it to both me and my family. It was the first time I suspected that my thinking might be unusual.

We had gathered over coffee at the kitchen table in my oldest sister's house. I was returning to Philadelphia from Iowa during a college break and a family visit. While I can't remember the exact subject of the conversation, I do remember that it was serious and rather philosophical, as it often was when my father was involved.

The moment that will remain forever imprinted in my memory was my father's reaction to hearing me describe my thoughts and feelings on the subject being discussed. He began to cry. As I was talking, a tear fell down his cheek. Then he began to weep quietly, tears streaming over his face.

I don't think I had ever seen my father cry before that moment. It seemed like an odd time to cry, since the subject wasn't necessarily one that would normally provoke such a reaction. My family was bewildered.

He began to explain, quietly. He said that I was a "thinker" a very deep thinker, someone who feels deeply and compassionately. He had also been listening to the tapes of my songs that I had recorded and sent to him.

"I understand your songs," he said to me. "I get them."

That caused the entire family to fall awkwardly silent.

At that moment, I felt as though I had somehow made my father proud of me, and that he was overcome with joy at knowing that his son was not an idiot or a follower, but an intelligent, caring person who thought deeply about the world and the people in it.

But now, many years later, I believe he was overcome with sadness.

Sadness because he knew all too well what my life had in store for me. He knew from experience what it was like to think and feel so much that it could become debilitating. He felt the suffering; as only a parent can — of what his son would go through, and he wept for me. Maybe he also wept over the responsibility of having handed down such a gift and such a curse.

The "family curse," as my middle sister Andrea and I affectionately call it.

Thinking too much.

Being a parent myself, I know my father's agony all too well. I hope to God that neither of my children inherits this particular curse and becomes a prisoner of anxiety and depression like their father. Even that fear is yet another source of anxiety, and another example of thinking way too damn much.

Every parent worries about their children, about what could be, and what is to come. Don't they? We would all gladly suffer their pain for them, if it were possible. But it is a burden for them to bear.

As for feeling too much, well, I've got that covered too.

I've always been well endowed with the gift of empathy. Emotional or affective empathy is my specialty. I tend to share the emotions and feelings of others, especially those who are suffering. Recognizing the pain and suffering of others, is unfortunately, quite easy for me. While it's entirely possible that this is a false perception on my part, I really don't think it is.

Empathy of course makes life much harder. It would be a lot easier if all I cared about was myself.

Empathy can be good too; and I mean really good. If you've ever been to a concert and experienced thousands of people singing together, and felt that overwhelming togetherness that music can bring, then you have experienced a magical form of empathy.

It also happens to me when I occasionally attend church. The vastness of souls, desperate, chanting, singing, begging for forgiveness, and the thought of God knowing all of their, all of our, troubles, sins, pain, fear, and joy, all mashed together, is an empathy overload for me.

I don't go to church very often, but when I do, I usually cry.

I Can't Let Go

"I can't let go, something's wrong, something's right."
-from the song "Can't Let Go"
-me

I can't seem to just let go or simply be. Now, more than ever, especially now, I am afraid. I live my life in fear—fear of the unknown—and it consumes me daily. I am afraid of every experience, whether it be walking the dog, going to work, taking my son to school, or of course waking up in the morning to face a new day of hell. I was never much afraid of anything before. I've always felt somewhat indestructible, confident even. I felt the need to find unusual experiences, and sometimes risky ones. I welcomed them. I chased them. I lived for them. I jumped trains. I climbed and leaped off of cliffs. I bound and danced down spring snow covered mountains. I hiked in the wilderness. I hitchhiked across the country. I performed music in front of audiences. I quit my job, grew my hair out, bought a VW bus and travelled around the country. I backpacked through Europe for 8 weeks. I was homeless. I was a middle school teacher for God's sake. I sought out adventure. I was brave and fearless. But this, this is different, this is a fear I've never felt before. This is pure relentless crippling fear.

And now I wonder if I will ever get myself back. Is this going to be me for the rest of my life? Will I ever not be afraid again? How long can I bear this? How long can a person live like this? I am suffering, and it feels as though it is all self-inflicted. What a cruel joke. What a pathetic joke I am.

The worst part of this calamity is that I feel as though my anxiety is written all over my face and that my fear is shouting from my eyes. People must know. They must see that I am afraid. They must sense my anxiety before I even speak. They seem to pull away from me, to shun me, as though I am a leper, an outcast, something unwanted. I feel exposed. I feel marked. I feel ashamed.

Soul

"You don't have a soul. You are a soul. You have a body."
-C.S. Lewis

"No good deed goes unpunished" is a twist on the idea that good deeds will be rewarded and bad deeds will be punished. It can be traced back to a 12th-century writing, a sign outside the EPA office during the Reagan administration, and even to the Broadway musical Wicked. I've always wanted to be "good" or do "good." I'm not sure why, nor would I ever say I was successful, either. Nevertheless, there has always been this other consciousness looking over me, evaluating my goodness. It is watching me, telling me "I should do this or that," or "what if this happens," or "shouldn't I be doing this instead of that?" It criticizes me, evaluates me, and tells me what is best. It even tells me what order things should be done in to maximize efficiency of time and effort. It questions my goodness and tells me that I don't deserve to be happy. It was always manageable, but always there. It ate away at my confidence and limited me.

Intense self-awareness, coupled with obsession and the need for perfection, in my case often led to dissatisfaction and eventually guilt. This self-critical awareness and guilt are a family trait, passed down from generation to generation in my family. I saw it in my mother and her sisters, and I see it in my sisters as well. I was never confident about myself. I never felt good about myself. I never knew a sense of belonging or of being comfortable. I have battled with this self-consciousness my whole life. Even as a child, I remember arguing with it at times.

All of these things have intensified one-hundred-fold in the last year, as severe anxiety has taken hold. My life has become a battle, a battle that I am mostly losing. Anxiety and depression are my enemies, and they are winning.

When I was younger, I mistakenly thought that this hyper self-awareness was my soul, or possibly God. Now I'm sure that it is not, but rather a defect of my mind that keeps me from truly living. It is this inner conversation, this constant voice, that is always there. Sometimes I wish it would just leave me the hell alone. I'm sure everyone has something like this to some degree, don't they? Hopefully not to the extreme that I am so fortunate; or unfortunate—to possess. Mine overwhelms me to the point where I've forgotten how to just live.

Einstein once said, "Life is like riding a bicycle. To keep your balance, you must keep moving." I'm not moving right now. I've lost my balance, fallen off my bicycle, and skinned my knees and palms. I've got to get back on that bicycle and keep moving. I recently bought a bike to symbolize this notion—and to some degree, my retirement. I received a gift card for $125 from my school for 23 years of service. Such a fitting reward for someone who lost just about everything from their teaching career. I thought, why not? A bike was a symbol of freedom for me as a child; maybe it will represent my release from teaching purgatory and celebrate my freedom. Let's face it, I'll try anything at this point to push anxiety and fear away.

The problem is that when I try going on bike rides, things are fine for a short distance, but when I ride too far from home, I get an anxiety attack and have to turn around. Pathetic! Evidently that old adage, "Once you learn how to ride a bike, you never forget," doesn't apply here. I taught myself how to ride a bike when I was eight years old. I just got on, fell off, and got back on again. Nobody taught me. It was in Florida, and it didn't take me long to get good. Riding a bike as a kid was freedom. Freedom to explore, take risks, travel to unknown lands. To ride down steep hills, take sharp turns, do tricks, pop wheelies, take jumps off curbs, brake hard and skid out to the side, find trails in the woods, make obstacle courses, and, of course, wipe out.

As a kid, I lived on my bike. I had some pretty awesome bikes. The Stingray was my favorite, with the banana seat and a sissy bar, and once, a five-speed shifter on the frame. I once had a purple sparkly banana seat that was boss. There's a picture of me at about age ten, sitting on my Stingray, nothing but shorts, with long blonde hair. I looked wild, confident, and strong. I remember my mom and I talking about my desire to grow my hair out during this time. She agreed, partly because I always put up a fuss about getting my hair cut and partly because of a really bad experience at the barber, which traumatized me. My mom told this butcher of a barber that I wanted only a trim, but he did the complete opposite and buzz cut me. I remember crying the whole time, and my mother being very angry with him.

It was the late '60s, early '70s; the Vietnam War was ongoing, and there were people protesting in the streets, many of them hippies with long hair. I saw them as heroes and wanted to be like them and look like them. I'm pretty sure that barber was not a supporter of long-haired protesters.

Anyway, I used to ride my bike everywhere. I would go out into unknown streets and neighborhoods. It didn't matter how far I went. I had no fear. Sometimes I would get lost and not know how to get back. Now, just riding half a mile away on a bike path fills me with fear and anxiety. I usually turn around and go home. I'm working on my distance. When I was a kid, I usually rode barefoot. Because I had unusually large feet, my feet would hang over the pedals quite a bit. This would occasionally cause me to scrape my big toes on the pavement while pedaling, ripping the flesh off in a gruesome, painfully bloody mess. I would do this several times in my childhood, just having healed only to do it again. You'd think I would have learned from the first time. Life lesson number one: never ride a bicycle barefoot.

I've always placed a great deal of value on having a soul. But what do I mean by a soul? In its most complex form, the soul for me is what gives life meaning. It is something that lives separate from the body, mind, spirit, and emotions. It is the part of me that seeks meaning and goodness. In its purest form, it might be love, or perhaps expressed through love, kindness, compassion, and art of all kinds. For me, discovering my soul has been a lifelong journey. An imperfect journey of seeking truth, expression, love, generosity, giving, and, I guess, doing good. The soul is the essence of you, that which connects us with others in deep ways. It is where love resides.

The conundrum is that one has to have a certain amount of self-awareness to realize one's soul. If you simply exist for the physical pleasures of this world, then you are, by default, not aware of your soul, and probably much happier, I might add. It is an awareness of something so deep that it cannot be explained. You either have it, or you don't, I think. Therefore, it is a curse and a blessing.

At this point, you may be saying to yourself: "What an idiot you are! You are a self-righteous, self-important narcissist who thinks you are better than most people, and the rest of us are unimportant. You and your stupid soul, heh!" Well, you may be partially correct, but I must also say that if you are reading this book, you are most likely aware of what I am speaking of. I do not think I am better than anyone, just different from most. I am also aware that my super-sonic self-awareness may be what I mistake for a soul, but I think not. I feel the connections that I have made with other humans; while few comparatively—are deep and beyond mere friendship or love. It is as though those feelings transcend time.

This may account for the fact that I have very few friends, something that makes me feel dreadfully inadequate, especially in my later years. This may also be due to the fact that I moved around a lot and was not able to establish close, enduring relationships with others. Frankly, I have just had a hard time making friends. There are very few people in this world who are willing to talk deeply and with whom I feel a true connection. Nevertheless, the way that I think about life feels different from many people I have met.

This is all speculation and possibly bullshit, and I am sure a good psychologist could diagnose me with some malfunction. But doesn't the fact that the medical field of psychology exists, and that diagnoses have been established, show that others feel this way too? Isn't psychology merely a way of explaining the ways different people think and move about this earth in a physical sense? It is when we fail to function properly within our society that we are recognized as being ill. I doubt the science of psychology takes into account the existence of the soul.

Has it ever occurred to anyone that society might not be right? That society, the soulless and the norm, are the truly sick people of the world? They hide behind the mundaneness of their everyday life, following the expected ways of societal living; religion, patriotism, work, money, consumerism, etc. They watch nighttime network television shows like Survivor or Matlock, or some other shit. They accept everything that is put before them as what life should be because thinking about the meaning of their existence takes too much time and effort; and is a very dangerous endeavor indeed. I have never been able to accept these things. I have strived to live outside of these traps while at the same time wishing that I could only be normal and free from these constraints. A paradox, to be sure, and the root of many of my problems.

Simple things, like holidays that give people warm thoughts, inspire decorations, and all those other trappings, do not move me. They have the opposite effect, making me feel even more apart from others, melancholic, and even hopeless. I am at the same time horrified by, and envious of, normalcy. I've often wondered whether cases of insanity are really people who see the world as it truly is—absurd and really fucked up, and can't deal with it anymore. Don't be fooled: there are millions of people out there dealing with some sort of mental strife. Some more severe than others, some like mine, and some with their own version of hell.

Simply know that I am on the journey of self-discovery and am writing down these discoveries as I go, in hopes of better dealing with my condition of life and maybe even striking a chord with you, good reader.

Does the soul live on after death? There is some science that goes both ways on this question. I have read a few articles on "the existence of the soul," and it seems understandably inconclusive. Much like the existence of God or a god. Because aren't the two, God and the soul; forever intertwined, interconnected? There is no proof. Faith! Faith is all we have to explain the unknown, the things that we, or I desperately want to know and understand.

If there were certain proof of God and the soul, it would surely blow the roof off human existence. Knowing for sure that your soul would live on and that God existed in some neat, graspable form, complete chaos! Or complete rebellion. I wonder how many people believe that they have a soul. Do they simply think as deeply as their religious upbringing allows and settle for the little information they are given? I suspect that most people are simple creatures, and lucky they are to be so. Do they think about life deeply, or do they just take what comes, living in the moment as it were?

What if, at the end of the day, each person got a score for how meaningful their day was? How much they contributed to the well-being of others, or how little they adversely affected others—a soul score, if you will. I have a feeling that, in the end, it wouldn't have much of an effect on human behavior. I don't feel confident that people actually care about meaning and purpose in life on a grand scale. Nor do I hold most people in high esteem; or like very many people, for that matter.

I give myself a soul score every freaking day, and several times a day. This is my life. I am always self-evaluating myself, my purpose, and the meaning of my existence. But it comes from me, not some omnipotent source. All this does is mess me up. It's like a life constipated. Everything is thought about, not just lived. Nothing is done without supervision by this conscious entity, or "soul," or whatever the hell it is. There is no sheer pleasure or joy.

I wish this consciousness would leave me the hell alone. Get out! Stop it! I don't want you in there anymore. I hate you! I'm sorry. Please forgive me. I didn't mean it.

Some say the soul is merely physical brain patterns, and that emotions and feelings are just part of the brain's functions. I find it hard to imagine that everything about me is purely physical, but I would imagine that if you believed this, life might be easier. Ignorance is bliss, after all. Ignorant people scare me. People who seem to live their lives only in the physical world scare me a great deal. I envy them, I despise them, I admire them, and I avoid them. They are not for me. They are beyond control, and I do not like things that are out of control.

I believe that most people have a soul, although it depends on the day. Not a religious thing so much as a spiritual part of them that is separate from their physical being. I believe some people's souls are more developed than others. A friend of mine told me about a theory suggesting that only about 25% of the humans on this earth actually have souls. The rest of the human race are just empty, devoid of soul—humans walking around not thinking too deeply or having any regard for other humans. An accidental life, if you will. People who do not seek a deeper connection or are aware of a spiritual world. A simple life, and oddly ironic—something that would bring me great relief.

Unconsciousness.

This notion that: 75% of humanity might not have a soul—is a curious idea that I find both fascinating and frightening. If it were true, it would make a great deal of sense to me. I used to believe that many of the people I met did not have souls. I'm a little more forgiving in my older years. I can think of a few people who definitely appear to not have souls. Maybe their souls are just bad souls. Who knows?

It doesn't take long to discover who has a soul. Sometimes you can almost feel their soul, and you have an instant connection that is undefinable. I think of people with souls as people who have something about them that is intangible and unimaginable. It is just there—undefinable but felt. I sense this in people I meet casually and in people I have known for many years. There are many pretenders, for sure. People who think they are soulful—or perhaps their soulfulness is a different kind than what I am sensitive to. These pretenders can be easily found out by me.

When I am around people with souls, it just feels different. They are connected to something bigger. Of course, I could be just making this up in my mind and being a judgmental prick, but I don't think so.

Being aware of myself and thinking about life is something I've done since I was a child. I've always felt that it was important to do "the right thing," whatever that was or is. Not simply accepting and consuming, but questioning and analyzing life, searching for some meaning or importance; hoping that life has a deeper purpose than just serving oneself. While I am quite sure that much of life is random and ambiguous, I also believe that one's purpose should be to do good.

What if being dishonest and trampling over other people to get what you want has no different outcome than trying to be kind, fair, and honest? Notice I said *try*. I'm no saint. But then I don't think for one minute that I will be rewarded at the end of my life for any good that I have done, or for the bad that I have avoided doing. I don't have some religious sense of being rewarded by eternal bliss in heaven or any other such thoughts. Nor do I believe that I will suffer eternal damnation in hell for all of the "not-so-good" things that I have done or will do.

I do, however, subscribe to karma or, to put it in Christian terms, "as you sow, so you shall reap." In fact, I used to introduce my sixth-grade students to the idea of karma in the hopes of maybe making them think about their lives a little more deeply. I did not spend any time at all on the idea, but rather just a quick mention of the word, followed by, "Since you are now aware of karma, you will start to see it more and more frequently in your life." It was my way of casting a little spell on my students, a good little spell, if you will, to maybe get them to think about the consequences of their actions.

I'm sure dogmatic religious people would call me out as evil or the devil for saying such things about the soul. However, I must insist that religion does not enter into my beliefs about the soul. I mean let's face facts, people can justify just about anything in the name of their God, including genocide and injustice.

My father was no slouch when it came to knowledge about religion. After all he did have an honorary PHD from Yale in religious studies. He knew the history, real sources of information from Latin texts, and the writings of many, many scholars and religious figures from the beginnings of Christianity. Once, when I was confronted by a "born again" Christian who spoke of eternal damnation, of not claiming Jesus Christ as "one's personal savior," and of the eventual judgment day or "rapture" when all would be rewarded and/or punished, I got freaked out and very frightened. So, I went to ask my dad about this rapture thing.

My dad's response went something like this: First of all, he said, the people telling you this are people who take the Bible literally and do not understand the real meaning of the text or the historical context in which this scripture was written. Secondly, he stated that he believed no loving God would condemn and torture people in such a way as described by this interpretation. And lastly, he believed that this life we are living now is, in fact, "hell." It is where we do our suffering and commit horrible acts against each other, as witnessed by the acts of men and women throughout history up until this very day.

While some may say this was a horrible thing to tell a young, impressionable teenager, I have to say it made perfect sense to me. It actually made me feel better. Was this a self-prophecy, or was it just the damn truth? I actually think it is the most reasonable and sensible thing I have ever heard about religion and God.

This reminds me of a funny thing my dad used to do. When Jehovah's Witnesses would knock on our door, instead of sending them away, he would invite them in. He loved to school them on scripture and the Bible. His knowledge was so vast that these poor souls would end up leaving our house flustered, confused, and dismantled. It was fun to watch and very informative.

So, back to the original question: Why do I do this? I do it because I have no choice, it is simply the way my mind works. It's hard to live like this, especially when your conscience; or soul, is watching over you, scrutinizing you every minute of every hour of every day. Do most people try to be kind, fair, and honest? Maybe they don't think about it as much as I do, and it just comes naturally for them. I mean, really, if you thought about the infinite number of ways that what you do on a daily basis affects the lives of others, you might be a little anxious yourself, don't you think? One cannot do this and live happily. You have to put these thoughts out of your mind, if you even have them at all—or you will be paralyzed. Now you get a small glimpse into what it might be like to have severe anxiety.

I Know the Story

"Pain is inevitable. Suffering is optional."
-Haruki Murakami

I am neurotic, it seems. "Thoughts and behaviors deviant from social norms," according to the Urban Dictionary. "Often maladaptive." Evidently the term is no longer used in psychiatric diagnosis—probably because it is too general. On the other hand, I am very critical of others. I am a judgmental prick, as it were. But I am a very accurate judgmental prick, and my judgments have been proven correct many times. My wife will sometimes ask me about my opinion on people because she knows firsthand of this deadly accuracy that I possess.

Being right about a person's character does not give me satisfaction or pleasure. It does, of course, limit my interactions with people that I feel are simply not worth the trouble. I do not, therefore, have many casual friends or acquaintances. While probably not very healthy, it simplifies things. Less clutter. I guess I find most people shallow and uninteresting. (Did you know that only 30–50% of people have an internal monologue? This, according to psychologist Russell Hurlburt's research.)

Nothing is new. It's like I'm watching a movie for the umpteenth time—I know the ending, I know how it all turns out. I get bored with people, or I've seen their story many times. Much like my story, I get bored with myself as well. They all end the same. I guess I should play along and enjoy the story. Even when talking about important issues, I just end up feeling uninterested or hopeless.

I find that as I get older, very few things seem important. We're all just biding our time, taking up space, going through the motions, playing the game of life, and pretending it all matters. We're the mouse on the wheel, in the cage. Life is rather pointless and futile, because we're all fucking doomed anyway. Optimism is also not one of my strong points.

The Fear of Happiness/Death

"I think I'm afraid to be happy because whenever I get too happy, something bad always happens."
-Charlie Brown

I don't believe that many people really think too much about their exit from this world: why would they? It's not a very pleasant thing to think about. When I was young, I felt immortal. Death was never something I considered much. But as I get older, the idea of dying creeps into my thoughts more and more. I wonder: will my death be clean and quick, like a massive heart attack? Messy and quick, like a car accident? Long and painful, like anxiety and depression—or Alzheimer's Disease? On and off again, like cancer: cancer, treatment, remission, cancer, and death? Slow, long, and lonely, watching everyone else you've ever loved die while you, the bitter, depressed, miserable one, outlasts them all? There is an infinite number of ways one can go.

What's contrary or backwards—about me is that I have always been more afraid of happiness than death. Afraid that happiness is an omen of horrible things to come. I've never been able to enjoy the moment and just be happy, because that's when tragedy can most certainly strike, tragedies like disease, the death of a loved one, or something else unbearable. Happiness can be ripped away in an instant.

As it turns out, there is actually a phobia in psychology called cherophobia: the fear of happiness. While it is not currently recognized as a clinical disorder, several studies have begun to validate its existence scientifically. I have been aware of it for quite some time, unfortunately. Adding to all of this, I find happiness (and life) to be very uncontrollable and unpredictable. Being happy is the ultimate state of vulnerability. I think that the obsessive-compulsive part of me is unable to cope with the uncontrollable and the vulnerability. I want things to be neat, controllable, and predictable. If I keep myself relatively free of happiness, then life will be more predictable and controllable, and there will not be so much to lose.

It is not my goal in life to be happy, never has been. Happiness or being happy is overrated in my opinion. Many people I know seek to be happy and place a great deal of importance on it. Many come up woefully short and are of course constantly disappointed. Anyone who seems overly happy to me is for sure someone to be avoided at all cost. They are either faking it, shallow, or overcompensating for something terrible. When someone asks me if I'm happy, I never know what to say. It's a confusing question to answer and I never do have a good answer.

Researcher and well-known author Brené Brown distinguishes the state of happiness from joy and contentment. She describes happiness as "feeling pleasure, often related to the immediate environment or current circumstances." Brown defines joy as having a higher intensity than happiness: "an intense feeling of deep spiritual connection, pleasure, and appreciation." On the other hand, contentment is the "feeling of completeness, appreciation, and 'enoughness' that we experience when our needs are satisfied." My father used to say, "It is better to be content than happy." I am afraid that his words may have had too much influence over me, as I have always subscribed to that very notion. Happiness is fleeting, while contentedness can last longer. Happiness is cheap and easy to come by; contentedness has to be worked for. For me, contentment is having a meaningful purpose in life, doing good or something that benefits others, feeling a sense of accomplishment, and making deep personal connections.

This is not to say that I have never felt happiness. I have, and sheer joy as well, but not without caution. Hemingway wrote, "Happiness in intelligent people is the rarest thing I know." I guess that's my problem, I'm just too damn intelligent to be happy. (sarcasm here) There has also always been a certain amount of guilt that I associate with happiness, because I'm not quite sure that I really deserve it.

My fear of happiness is similar to my fear of love and friendships. Becoming too close to someone and loving someone makes me vulnerable to loss. And loss of love would be too much to bear. I believe that this is why I have had such a hard time being a husband and a parent. I mean, let's face it: becoming a father or mother is the ultimate leap of faith. To have and love your children is the most wonderful yet most vulnerable thing a human can do, in my opinion. I could not bear losing my wife, son, or daughter. I think it would destroy me. It is uncontrollable, and that's why I should have never had children. Big mistake! A big wonderful, messy mistake. Love, it's a risky and dangerous business.

It's possible that my fear of happiness may have had its beginnings in the practice of my family moving around quite a bit. The idea that I shouldn't get too happy or attached to friends and community, because we're most likely going to move again and I'll lose those friendships. I became subconsciously guarded, if you will. Funny; it would seem like the Gods have played their tricks on me and given me the things that I fear the most: a wonderful wife and two lovely children. Insidious, isn't it?

A Revolution

"You say you want a revolution, we all want to change the world"
-Lennon and McCartney

Being a conscious human means thinking too much, constantly questioning and justifying your life and well-being. You see the injustices, sorrow, pain, corruption, and greed in the world. You try to find meaning in a reality that often feels senseless.

You wrestle with your own fortune: a beautiful home, plenty of food, clean water, freedoms we take for granted—while much of the world lives in fear, hunger, disease, war, and violence too awful to imagine.

How do we reconcile this? How can I live in my safe little bubble, enjoying my comfortable life while so many are suffering? How can anyone be happy or content in a world like this?

A revolution would be a start. A big, unapologetic revolution where people have simply had enough—storming the Bastille, and by that, I mean the White House and every other seat of injustice and corruption in this world.

A world where the ultra-rich are held accountable, forced to pay for the good of everyone. I'm not talking about the storming of the White House for a single person's agenda, if you know what I mean. I mean a rebellion against power, greed, big business, and corruption.

A complete wiping of the slate. An overthrow of the oligarchy we mistakenly call a democracy. Power returned to the people. A new beginning, where government serves the people, not billionaires and millionaires. The start of treating everyone with care, fairness, and responsibility. A start of providing a quality education for everyone, and where healthcare is a right not a privilege.

It's a pipe dream, I know. Perhaps contrary to human nature, for good to truly win out.

As you may or may not know, the history of this country is built on the backbone of indentured service, slavery, oppression, and deception. The winners write the history books, which is why most people know so little about the truth.

Yes, a revolution is something I would find deeply compelling; worthwhile. Because really, it's all bullshit. This life we've created here in America: entertainment for the masses, sedating ourselves with work, sports, beauty, beer, television, Netflix, and social media. A false narrative, an illusion that anyone can truly "make it" here. The dumbing and numbing of the populace, to the point where people believe the very ones who oppress them are acting in their best interest, or that there's nothing they can do about it.

It's a dull time in history. I call it the era of apathy; and I don't excuse myself from it. I've always felt I should have been born in a time when history was being made. Perhaps during a world war, or a revolution—a time that demanded conviction, survival, grit, and action. A time of instinct.

The only thing that could make things right here is a complete overhaul. It would be messy, brutal even, but it would capture my interest. The injustices, the misuse of power and wealth, they are glaringly obvious in our history, yet the majority remain ignorant. Our education offers only a patriotic, "good guy vs. bad guy" version of events, and somehow, we are always the good guys.

I wish I were ignorant of all this, like most people. That would ease my anxiety immensely. But again, nothing is too big to worry about when you have severe anxiety. Ignorance is bliss. Right? What's most disturbing to me is that some people choose to remain ignorant. They don't want to think about the children who die in mines so that they can have a battery for their cell phone, or electric car. They don't want to think about the sweatshops in poor countries that make most of their clothing. They don't want to believe that money and power supersedes justice. They think that the dark part of history is not worth learning. It's too upsetting. Besides it will just make me feel bad and who needs to feel bad? This I think is the current normal.

From the outside, I might seem the epitome of normal: I live in the suburbs, I'm married, I have a child who plays sports and is very active. I drive an average car. I carry way too much credit card debt. I appear, fucking normal.

But I am not. I believe most people are not like me, and I wish I were like them. They seem so happy in their ignorance. I look at them and wonder what is wrong with me. It feels as if I am unable to participate, as though I'm looking through a window at life happening all around me. My nose pressed against the glass, it's steaming up. I write "Can I come in?" but I can't. Ironically, the window isn't locked, but I still can't enter.

Starlings

"Now panic beats and flutters inside my skull like a flock of starlings locked in an attic."
-Stephen King

Today is a gray, blustery day, and I'm having trouble getting out of bed—as usual. A flock of starlings just landed on the roof and began pecking around the edges of our skylight. I've never seen anything like it. What is this Alfred Hitchcock's *The Birds?* That movie scared the crap out of me as a child. I threw a towel up at the glass and it scared them away. What an ominous, disconcerting start to the day. Really.....what an odd occurrence.

Starlings are dirty birds, in my opinion. Not native to the United States, yet they've thrived to the point that other, more beautiful birds seem increasingly scarce. All the European starlings in North America supposedly descended from about a hundred birds released in New York's Central Park in the early 1890s. They were set loose by a group that wanted America to have every bird mentioned by Shakespeare. Now starlings are everywhere. Thanks a lot. As T.S. Eliot said, "Most of the evil in this world is caused by people with good intentions."

An occasional leaf blows past my bedroom window. I still can't seem to get out of bed. I should eat something, but I have no appetite. The thought of falling asleep here and never waking up feels comforting. I'm tired. Anxiety wears a person down, mentally and physically. It's difficult to get out of bed when you have nothing to look forward to but suffering.

But I'm suffering in bed as well. Here it comes—that rush of anxiety, that awful feeling of dread, shame, and fear.

Time to get up.

Reflections on Getting Old

" Growing old is mandatory, but growing up is optional."

-Walt Disney

By the way, let me just clear things up right away. Getting old pretty much sucks. No one has ever, to my knowledge, written a proper guide to getting old that tells the harsh reality of what to expect as you age. Some possible titles might be *Getting Old for Dummies*, or *Getting Old and Slowly Falling Apart*, or even *Nibbled to Death by Ducks*. Perhaps there aren't a lot of honest books on getting old because it's such an unpleasant subject for most people. Or perhaps, no one, including me, who is in the throes of getting older; wants to read such a book. In fact, there may be lots of books about getting old, but I've never sought them out. I don't want to sound like a complainer, but getting old has not been extremely rewarding for me, and I despise those books and articles about enjoying your elder years. Phillip Roth wrote, "Old age isn't a battle, old age is a massacre." I agree.

Here are just a few things from my observations that you should know about getting older. You sleep less; a lot less. I'm not sure why, but it is something you either have to accept, or suffer with. I am not a napper, like old people seem to do throughout the day. I never have been able to nap. You have more flatulence. Your hair gets gray and thinner, and the possibility of going bald is a scary reality. You wake up every morning stiff and sore. You have pains that you sincerely hope go away, because if they don't, you're probably going to need surgery. You might get any number of diseases. Your eyesight gets worse. Your hearing gets worse. Just the other day, I noticed that I had this constant ringing in my ears, tinnitus. I was worried, so I went to the doctor. He said, "Nothing abnormal; ringing in the ears happens when you get older. I have it myself." What the hell! Nobody tells you that your ears are going to constantly ring when you get older, and that this is something you have to learn to live with for the remainder of your life. Surely deafness is inevitable for me, having played loud guitar for much of my life.

Dental work. Lots of dental work. Expensive and painful dental work. You get much more sore from doing physical activities. You resent technology. You sometimes lose your lust for life. You get strange skin marks, and when you go to the dermatologist, you're pretty sure you've got skin cancer because you weren't really good about wearing sunscreen. By the way, going to the doctor is extremely risky and anxiety-inducing, because as you get older, the odds are in favor of disease. You are, after all, a machine that is slowly falling apart. How well you took care of your machine and kept up maintenance over the years sometimes determines how bad the repair bill will be. By repair bill, I of course mean the suffering. Old age is when the bill comes due for all of the things you've neglected or done to yourself when you were younger. You've had your fun; now it's time to pay up.

Possibly the worst and saddest fact about getting old is that you are no longer a viable sexual object to young, beautiful women. There will never be a passionate, torrid sexual encounter with another young woman again. Of course, I am married to a young, passionate, beautiful woman, so I guess it's some consolation, but still, the thought that I was attractive to other women was reassuring and stimulating, to say the least. It's nice to be desirable and wanted. Not anymore.

One of the most telling aspects of getting older is that you realize you are not immortal anymore, and that your time left on this earth is very limited. It's inevitable. The clock is ticking. And lastly, one of the really depressing parts of getting old is watching people you've known and some that you have loved throughout your life die.

I've noticed there are countless books and endless advice about retiring with financial security. But what percentage of people actually retire with "financial security"? What the Sam Hill does that even mean? What is security, anyway? A person with severe anxiety may not even know what it feels like to be secure. We should all be so lucky.

We're told to plan for the future when we're young. I didn't do that. I didn't plan for the next week; I just lived for the day.

There are also plenty of articles and books about how to reverse the damage you've done to yourself over the years, and how to live longer and be healthier. But there doesn't seem to be a practical book about what the average person should actually expect as they get older.

Being older also means you've acquired a lifetime of things, most of them useless and outdated. Your house is full of "things" that, I'm sure, were useful at one point. I think possessions are the beginning of the end. Owning things can stagnate a life. Buying a house, for example, as they say, is setting down roots. What a strange practice. That notion has always been contrary to my nature. I was raised to roam. My parents moved a lot. Somehow, I ended up thinking I should put down roots in Des Moines, Iowa, of all places. Of all the places in the world, I landed in Des Moines, Iowa. Random, right?

Songwriting and Suffering

"To live is to suffer, to survive is to find some meaning in the suffering."
-Friedrich Nietzsche

Writing a song sounds like such a wonderful thing to do, and it should be. Listen to what I've created; isn't it beautiful? Fa la la la la.

I used to write songs; music, lyrics, all of it. I think my best songs were the ones that seemed to flow out of me from some other place. I was merely the vessel. There was something otherworldly about feeling possessed in an instant of inspiration.

Some were band songs, and some were songs I recorded on my own, singing and playing every part except the drums. Writing songs and playing in bands was one of the most exciting and creative times of my life. I played guitar and sang. I recorded songs with my band and on my own.

Our band, 23 Lies, is on vinyl—what we used to call an album. I recorded several studio tapes of my own music and gave them away in the popular format of the day: cassettes.

I loved recording. I loved the control I had over the composition of the songs, and the precision with which you could shape dynamics and instrumentation. I used interesting recording techniques, like recording a guitar solo backward to get a super-psychedelic sound, or using a homemade amp that screamed out a gnarly distorted solo.

My solo band's name was Psychedelic Doo Doo, and that's exactly what it was: some psychedelic shit.

Playing live music was a little riskier and more chaotic, depending on the sound man and the moods of each band member. It also depended on how much each member drank or what drugs had been taken beforehand.

At the root of all things, I am a perfectionist; a trait I got from my mother, a disease that leads to great unhappiness, obsessive compulsion and anxiety as well. Music was not immune to this perfectionism. Playing live places a heavy burden on the audience's approval. When an audience is really into you, the feeling is a buzz like nothing else in the world. It's like an out-of-body experience. Conversely, it is a horrible feeling not to be liked by an audience. Both happened to me in my short-lived musical career.

While I usually enjoyed the interaction with the crowd and my bandmates, it was far from perfect. Lumpy, our drummer, would sometimes drink way too much and forget where he was. I would look back at him with disdain when he messed up and see that look in his eyes, that glazed-over, drunken look that said, "I have no idea where I am, and not the foggiest idea how to keep time or rhythm." When that happened, we were screwed.

Before one show, I took some sort of hallucinogen: something Charles, our singer, had given me. To this day, I do not know what it was. Things were going along fine when, all of a sudden, someone turned on a mirrored disco ball above us. At that point, I lost all sense of gravity and became weightless, unable to stand. Some part of my consciousness knew I had to keep playing guitar, so I lay down on the stage floor and finished the set. My bandmates stood over me afterward, wondering whether they should call an ambulance. I was incoherent but smiling ear to ear, in complete ecstasy, watching the disco-ball lights spin slowly around me. Someone helped me up, and I went for a cold February walk during the break, which somehow allowed me to finish the show.

At another show, after taking mushrooms, I saw three fairy girls dancing around me, magical and laughing. To this day, I think they were real.

Some shows had large audiences; some were hardly worth the drive. We once played a show in Perry, Iowa, during a brutal winter, and there were maybe three people in the audience. On the way home, I nearly died on the icy roads, doing a 360-degree spin in the middle of a two-lane highway. Another time, we played an amazing Halloween show in a large warehouse, opening for a crowd favorite, The Hollowmen. We were inspired, the audience was huge and excited, and then, during our last song, the police arrived and dispersed the crowd because there was no license for a show like that in the warehouse district.

As with anything, there was good and bad. We were reviewed in the paper, sometimes unfavorably, and audiences received us with reactions ranging from total inspiration to complete indifference. At one show, we had to ask the bartender to turn off the television because it was distracting from our performance.

There were many late nights and even more late-night drives. We hauled equipment up and down stairs, ate terrible food, drank too much, and took too many drugs. I had a flair for theatrics then—leaping off stages, jumping on tables, wind milling my arm to drive home a chord. One time, I smashed an old, worthless guitar I had stolen from a small shop, a despicable act I still feel awful about. But I did not even smash it properly. Instead of milking the destruction to a final climax the way my guitar heroes had, I lifted it over my head and brought it down in one clean blow. The sound ended abruptly, and the guitar shattered into a few large pieces. Ah well. It was my first and last attempt at smashing a guitar.

A friend of mine, the drummer for The Hollowmen, kept the neck of that guitar. He later died by suicide. He was an incredible drummer and a kind-hearted soul. Years later, I had his children as students in my sixth-grade classroom. He lived near my school, and I would often see him after work, walking his dog as I left the building. To this day, I feel I should have recognized his depression and anxiety. The last time I saw him, we had gone out to dinner with friends visiting from out of town. I should have noticed he was suffering. I should have talked to him, helped him somehow. Why didn't I recognize that he was in trouble? Sadness.

During this time, I was working full-time for an insurance company during the day and playing music as much as possible on the side. It was nice to finally make decent money and not live hand to mouth. I had a decent car and a hip apartment across from the Art Center. I met musical people, and my band was playing original music. I was writing the music for the band, and the lead singer wrote the lyrics. We played shows and became fairly well known locally.

There were plenty of girls, for sure. Unfortunately, I was not skilled in the girl department, even as a rock-and-roll guitarist. I often had to rely on a girl being forward with me, or "picking me up," as they used to say. Many of those girls were not desirable to me in the least, and I rarely took advantage of my status. Still, I partied, caroused, and lived the life of a rock-and-roller.

Then I met a girl. Isn't that always the case? Things changed when I met her. Her name was Moon. That's not really her name, but that's what I'll call her. We met late one night at a party and had a great conversation. She had jet-black hair and dark eyes. I found her very attractive, both physically and intellectually. We met again later at a bar, and that eventually led to a long-term relationship.

Let's face it: girls have always messed me up—or maybe distracted and confused me is more accurate. I fell hard for this girl, harder than I ever had before. She was not just any girl, but the kind who inspired songs, desperation, longing, and ultimately tragedy. I was powerfully attracted to her in every way. It was a deep but doomed love—at least for me—one that had nowhere to go.

She gave me my first journal, and that inspired me to write. I was relatively young and, to be sure, overly dramatic. Of course, I didn't know that at the time. I even asked her to marry me. She said she "couldn't," but I think she wanted to. I always wondered about that response. It wasn't no. It was, "I can't." Why couldn't she? Maybe she had dreams and aspirations that marriage would have interfered with. Maybe she just didn't love me enough. Maybe it wasn't meant to be. Maybe I wasn't good enough for her, or not from the proper background. She came from a very wealthy family, and I was definitely not from that side of town. We stayed together for two years.

Regardless, it all came to a screeching halt when I slept with another girl, quit my job, climbed into my VW bus, drove around the country, got a girl pregnant, and got married against my better judgment. I sometimes wonder what would have happened if Moon and I had gotten married. A fork in the road. Ambiguity.

Perhaps the woman I loved was drawn to me as an artist, but the artist in me was fading. Yes, I was a songwriter and a guitarist in a band. I was writing what I believed were really good songs—musically and lyrically unique songs. It was great while it lasted, but over time I stopped. Playing music and writing songs wore on me. It would have required a commitment of flesh I was not able to give.

I didn't write soulless, meaningless songs. I wrote deeply felt songs, songs that took a great deal out of me. It took a toll. For some reason, I couldn't let go and allow the music to take me where it wanted to go. Why? Perhaps I mistakenly thought I could control that life. The life of a musician was clearly beyond control.

As a songwriter, I felt isolated in a surreal world of self-awareness and observation. I couldn't observe life, write songs about it, and honestly participate in it at the same time. It seemed impossible to me. For some reason, I gave up—or gave in. It is strange that I thought living a normal life would make those feelings of isolation and intensity disappear. It didn't. Not at all. And by failing to commit to the life of a musician and songwriter, I may have missed the only life I was truly made for.

I regret not taking that fork in the road sometimes. By now, I might be dead, semi-successful, or who knows what. "We only regret the chances we didn't take, the relationships we were afraid to have, and the decisions we waited too long to make." I think giving up music….stopping the writing and the playing, is one of my biggest regrets.

By the way, I still see that "song girl" around town once in a while. Des Moines is after all a small city and dare I say a bit incestuous even? I think she is happily married. My desire for her was a bit out of control, and I may have been a little drunk on unfulfilled longing. Desire can be a confusing emotion, to say the least. It can trick us and make us feel desperate sometimes. I wrote a song during that time aptly titled "Sister Desire."

Is it possible that rich people mostly marry other rich people? Is there some unwritten social requirement? Is this how the rich stay rich? Everyone stays in their social class. No marrying down.

Being rich is a condition I struggle to relate to. I know that sounds judgmental, and it is, but there is some truth to the differences between the rich and the middle class. We think about things differently. We have different values, values that sometimes conflict. We move in different social circles, and we have very different experiences that shape how we see the world.

One of my favorite authors, D. H. Lawrence, explored love between the working class and the upper class in *Lady Chatterley's Lover*, as did many other writers, including Edith Wharton in *The Age of Innocence*, Emily Brontë in *Wuthering Heights*, and Jane Austen in *Pride and Prejudice*, to name just a few of my favorites. In some ways, those differences in experience can feel irreconcilable and extremely difficult to overcome.

Don't get me wrong, she was, and is, a beautiful person. I guess there is never any shortage of tragic love stories in this world, real or imagined.

Of course, most of my favorite songwriters are either dead or writing really shitty songs. Think about it: how many great songs were written by people who were happily married and living normal lives? Getting married and having children does not fit well with writing good songs. You can't be a settled, happy, contented person and still write honestly about the realities of life. It doesn't work. The two don't go together. At least not successfully.

Who wants to listen to someone who is completely happy and content with life? Not me. In my opinion, songwriting has to be deep and suffered for. Sometimes I miss the songwriting days of my past life; that creative, self-absorbed, self-important, super-critical runaway train of a life. It feels as though a part of me died without my ever really noticing.

Avoidance and Worry

"I sometimes worry that I've forgotten what I was worrying about."

-me

You know how people purposely avoid thinking about certain things because the answers might be too much to bear? Those thoughts cross our minds, but we hold them at bay or push them aside until one day they break us open.

Thoughts like: Who am I, and what the fuck am I doing? Am I a good person? Will my children be OK? Will they be safe and happy? Do they feel loved? Am I raising them well? Does my wife still love me? Does she find me attractive? What do people really think of me? Does my life have meaning? Am I content? What does it even mean to be content? Should I be doing more for the good of humanity? Is my perception of reality even real? Does anything really matter? Does anything make a difference?

My anxiety is intensifying as I write this. I haven't even mentioned money, which would unleash a whole other set of thoughts and questions.

Here is something else absurd that I worry about. My mother and father are both dead, my father for quite a long time now, and my mother for about five years. When I stop to think about them, as I am doing now, I become incredibly sad. I feel the nostalgia of our family and the void their deaths have left in my life. They were so understanding and supportive of me. I am crying as I write this, and I miss them terribly. I cry quite easily these days.

I have to push those thoughts and memories aside. I have to push away the questions I still have about our relationship because they are unbearable. But the strangest part is that I worry I do not think about them enough. It is as if their eternal lives somehow depend on my remembering them, and I have not done a very good job of that.

Clearly, I think too much.

The Joy of Climbing Trees

"One could do worse than be a swinger of birches."
-Robert Frost

As I was describing my family background to my psychiatrist, he replied, "You've been dealt a nasty soup of psychological shit." I appreciated his humor and honesty and knew right away that he was the shrink for me.

By the way, he was not my first psychiatrist. I met my first one in a moment of sheer terror. I was at the end of my rope, coming unglued in my classroom during a break between classes, in the midst of what I later realized was an extreme panic attack. I found a doctor, called, begged to come in, drove to his office, and filled out paperwork, all within the span of a lunch hour.

When I walked into that office, I was shivering, convulsing, and incoherent. The doctor was kind enough to see me in the middle of that horror. He suggested that I immediately take a leave of absence from teaching and said he would help me fill out the paperwork for family medical leave. He advised me to inform my principal that I would be taking FMLA and leaving immediately. I got those twelve weeks of leave, which I believe saved my life.

Eventually, I went back to work for a short time and finished the school year. I liked that doctor. Whenever I asked him questions about what to do with my life, he would hand me the Magic 8 Ball. You know that toy that was popular when you were a kid in the '60s? A plastic sphere made to look like an eight ball, used for fortune-telling or advice. It was invented in 1950 and filled with alcohol and blue dye. There were twenty possible answers, some affirmative and some noncommittal, that appeared at the bottom. I got his point. There are no clear answers to life's questions.

Ambiguity strikes again. It is there all the time, every step of the way. You may not think about it much, but I sure do. The fact that your life is a book of blank pages, written as you go, with no direction—kind of like this book. No plot. No characters except the ones you write down as you live. Some people might think that's wonderful: I get to write my own story. I can be anything and do anything I choose. I don't look at it that way. In fact, it bothers me quite a bit. Maybe I don't like what I wrote in my open book of life. Maybe I didn't understand the rules. If I had known I could write anything on those blank pages, I might have done things differently. I may have felt empowered, not cautious and afraid.

Ah well, it doesn't matter after all. It's only life, right?

Wrong!

Some very intelligent people have written about fate and free will, or, as I call it, ambiguity. Baruch Spinoza said, "In the mind there is no absolute or free will; but the mind is determined to wish this or that by a cause, which has also been determined by another cause, and this last by another cause, and so on to infinity." In other words: random ambiguity.

That doctor, the Magic 8 Ball doctor, unfortunately moved to Colorado. I think he smoked weed and definitely approved of its use in treating mental disorders. I liked that doctor. He saved my life.

Fork in the road? Random?

As a child, you don't notice certain things about your parents. They seem perfectly normal because, to you, they are normal. You don't know any different; you have no other experience or framework from which to compare. It is simply how things are. Evidently, there was a great deal I didn't notice.

My father was manic-depressive, and my mother was an obsessive-compulsive perfectionist. Not good. Had I inherited only one of their traits, it might have been manageable. Unfortunately, I think I got all of their mental disorders. As you might imagine, that has been a difficult thing to overcome. But it was all normal to me, and I lived in it quite functionally for quite some time.

All that aside, a little background on my parents might be in order.

My father was born in 1921 in Oelwein, Iowa, and later moved to Cedar Falls when he was a young boy. He once told me that, looking back, he believed his mother had suffered from mental illness....probably depression. In his words, "the signs were there." She would sit in the dark for hours and go through long periods of withdrawal from life. His father worked for the Union Pacific Railroad and was away quite a bit.

Howard Benjamin was the youngest of three, with an older brother and sister, neither of whom I ever met. I never met his mother either. He did not share much about his upbringing, but I gathered that, because he was quite a bit younger than his siblings, he spent a great deal of time on his own, much like I did. There is a photograph of him as a child with a German shepherd that I love, but that is about the extent of the evidence I have of his childhood.

He attended college, as fate would have it, at a small school in Fairfield, Iowa, known then as Parsons College, where he met my mother. Incidentally, Parsons College was eventually transformed into Maharishi International University, which practices a "consciousness-based education" that includes Transcendental Meditation. Fairfield became a place of stark cultural contrast, as many wealthy practitioners of transcendental meditation moved there and mixed uneasily with the small-town locals. Let's just say things were tense for a while between the two groups. Eventually, relations thawed as the townspeople realized the benefits of jobs, money, and new residents flowing into their small town.

Many large mansions were built on the outskirts of Fairfield, and many modest homes adopted the architecture associated with transcendental meditation. For example, the front door of a home is often pointed east to greet the sunrise, and the roof may hold a golden ornament called a kalash, shaped like a Hershey's Kiss, supposedly meant to attract positive energy. The legendary American filmmaker David Lynch (*Blue Velvet, Wild at Heart, Elephant Man* and many others.) was very much into Transcendental Meditation. He often said that TM was the single most vital factor in his creative life. Lynch taught film classes as a frequent guest lecturer and established the David Lynch Graduate School of Cinematic Arts at Maharishi International University. He also founded the university's film department, and has pledged $1 million in scholarships to fund students looking to study at the university. I honestly never thought I'd mention David Lynch and Iowa in the same breath.

Anyway, back to our story.

My father was a tall man for his time, six feet tall—with dark black hair and blue eyes. He was a looker, for sure, a very handsome man. My mother was born in the small town of Donnellson, Iowa, in 1923 and had three older sisters. She was a brilliant child who played four instruments: the oboe, the viola, the piano, and the clarinet. She also played basketball in the days of six-on-six women's basketball.

Her father was a tall and foreboding man, very strict and demanding as well. I never met him, as he died rather early in life, but my mother often spoke of both her respect for him and her fear of him, as well as of the very high expectations he had for his daughters. My grandmother was a quiet, hardworking woman whom I knew only when I was very young. She had a huge garden and a cherry tree that I climbed and ate from as often as I could when we visited. She died when I was eleven. We lived a thousand miles away, and I never went to her funeral.

My mother was also tall for her time and was a strikingly beautiful woman with curly auburn-red hair.

They fell in love in their early twenties, and then World War II began. My father enlisted in the Navy and went off to officer training school. When he completed it, he returned to Iowa to marry my mother. My father once told me that "he didn't want to die a virgin." Maybe too much information.

The wedding pictures of him in his white Navy uniform and my mother in her gown are quite beautiful. They show only my mother's side of the family; my father's family is curiously absent.

My mother, of course, followed my father to his various bases and ports, including Seattle, San Diego, and San Francisco. One of her favorite places to live was San Francisco, where my father's ship was sent for repairs near the end of the war.

My father served as a lieutenant on the destroyer USS *Hutchins* and entered the war in November 1943. The ship first sailed to the Aleutians, where it came under numerous Japanese air attacks. It later took part in many battles in the South Pacific, including Iwo Jima and Okinawa. During some of these battles, it was under constant, intense attack. The ship was damaged in a collision with another vessel and was eventually struck by a Japanese suicide boat, forcing it back to Pearl Harbor for repairs. It later limped back to San Francisco and was then towed to Seattle for eventual decommissioning. Later, it was sold for scrap.

My father was deeply affected by his experiences in World War II. He saw men die. It was through those experiences that he became inspired to become a minister.

After the war, this calling took my parents first to Chicago for seminary and then to Yale University in Connecticut, where my father completed his honorary doctorate. They began their family in Detroit, where my father took his first pastoral position, thus beginning the many moves my family would make to different cities for his work. Both of my sisters were born in Detroit. I was not.

I do not remember much interaction with my mother and father as a child. They seemed very busy and so was I. Dinner was probably the only time in the day that we got together as a family, but my sisters were much older than me so they were not around much. In fact, I have very few childhood memories save for pictures of either of my sisters. I do remember my oldest sister Jenna having a collection of chewed gum on her headboard and her playing 45's on her record player. My favorite song was "Mr. Lonely" by Bobby Vinton. I guess I was doomed at a very early age. I have two early memories of my other sister, Andrea. One was the time I took one of her prized stuffed animals off her bed. She chased me around the house with bad intentions until I gave it back to her for fear of losing my life. I also remember a huge fight between my father and Andrea. Lots of shouting and doors slamming and me sitting on my mother's lap crying in terror.

My father came home every night after work, had a martini or bourbon and smoked a lot. That's about all I remember from my early childhood other than my own experiences.

My father was far from a perfectionist, unlike my mother, which made for a very difficult existence. (I know this firsthand.) He was the typical working father of the times. He did not clean, he did no laundry or cooking, he went to work and came home. That is to say uninvolved, while my mother was the typical mother of the times, stay-at-home, take care of the kids, do the cooking and laundry, etc. That is until I went to school, then she pursued her career in nutrition.

My mother had a serious mental breakdown before I was born. This occurred after the birth of my sister Andrea, who to this day claims that breakdown as the reason she is "so fucked up." Andrea has suffered with obsessive-compulsive disorder and at one time life-threatening anorexia. As a teenager it was scary for me to watch her waste away to under eighty pounds. She was hospitalized twice and had seizures from her anorexia. She has since gotten much better but still maintains a healthy OCD, by which she will probably live to be 120 years old. She and I are a lot alike in some ways. She worries me.

My mother was my savior, the love of my life. She loved me so much I can still feel it many years after her death. I miss her presence. She was pure love and good. But as children, we take our parents for granted and assume that they are all perfectly well and fine. I never noticed anything was wrong with either of my parents until I was an adult. Even now I look back and remember things that should have clued me in to their struggles.

My mother tried to kill herself once a few years after I had finished college and was working in Des Moines, Iowa. I found out purely by accident while talking to my father on the phone. He was agitated and somehow it came up in our conversation that he had found Mom passed out on the bed, an empty bottle of pills by her side. She was admitted to the hospital and eventually received electroconvulsive therapy. This seemed to help her for a good long while but eventually, many years later she suffered tragic extreme anxiety that led to her hospitalization in a very shady psychiatric hospital. The first day I walked in to this hospital to visit my mother I witnessed a man in a wheelchair with his hand up the robe of a female patient in a wheelchair who was incoherent. I yelled at that man, saying, "Hey, you stop it. You should be ashamed of yourself!" I was very angry and shocked. I think I scared the crap out of that guy. I told the nursing staff, but I'm not sure anything was done.

My mom eventually got much better and moved to a nursing home near my sisters. She lived a few years there and eventually died of colon cancer. My father, on the other hand, was a WWII veteran, smoked three to four packs of cigarettes a day, drank heavily, was a Presbyterian minister, met with Martin Luther King Jr., published an article in Look Magazine and lived life either full of manic zest and ferocity or debilitating depression. He could often times be found hibernating in his study in the dark, for months at a time. He then died painlessly in his sleep. Lucky bastard. Not that he didn't suffer a good share of his life.

I always thought I was closer to my dad, but it has come to light that, like most boys, I was ultimately closer to my mom in a deeper way. My dad was super interesting and quirky, brilliant and tortured. He had really great sayings that have stuck with me throughout life. I'm sure these sayings were not originally his, but still. Here are a few: "Live and learn." "Sheep dip!" "I guess you need to learn the hard way." "Never underestimate the stupidity of the American people." "If you haven't ever considered suicide, you're either lying or an idiot." "Never trust a man who doesn't drink." "Thank God for booze!" Later in life, as he was ailing from various maladies, he would say, "I feel like I'm being nibbled to death by ducks." One of my favorites was, "money isn't everything, but it sure do help."

I looked up to my father and wanted to be like him, and yet the father-son relationship in my case may have been a little detrimental to my overall mental health. I mean, who tells their kid, "if you haven't considered suicide, you're either a liar or an idiot?" I always felt like I was a "chip off the old block" and that we were very much alike. Maybe too much alike. He understood my suffering, but yet he may have had a great deal of influence in creating it as well. Insidious, huh?

You see, my dad was a thinker, a very deep thinker. He impressed upon me, not purposefully, the importance of thinking and not being one of the "mass idiots". He was extremely critical of others and usually cast a dark opinion on people as being simpletons, idiots, and fools. He did this all with sarcasm and wit, which our entire family was quite good at. This seeped into me throughout my early years and into my young adulthood. I strived to be like him, as most young boys do. Ah, the things we do for love. Or rather, the things love does to us.

From this deep thinking, intense sarcasm, and severe scrutiny of oneself and others, came a hyper self-aware young boy. I learned to never be comfortable with the normal enjoyment of the simple things, because I thought about them first instead of just feeling and experiencing them. My father's critical nature had seeped into the way I viewed and evaluated myself and the world around me. I couldn't just be; I had to justify myself, and ask myself if I was being one of those fools.

I don't blame either of my parents for anything. They did the best they could and loved all their children. As a father, I know that it is pretty hard to not mess up your children either through genes, or parenting, or both. As with most parents (I think), I am extremely afraid that I have done things that will cause problems later on in my children's lives. I tried to do my best, and hope they can overcome the bad and remember the good. Parenting sucks!

I was the youngest of three children, with two older sisters who were quite a bit older than me. Andrea was seven years older, and Jenna was nine years older. I felt adored by my family, being the youngest, and the only boy. I was a bit spoiled. At the same time, I was often left to my own devices. I think that's typical for the youngest child; by then, parents are fairly confident the kid will survive and figure things out.

Here are some things I remember from my childhood.

Running around barefoot and half-naked most of the time, playing

Tarzan. My Zorro plastic doll, which I accidentally left on my dad's bumper and never saw again. My toy machine gun and plastic Buck knife. Riding on the back of a friend's bike, falling off, and breaking my collarbone. I didn't get a cast, which would have been cool; but instead had to wear a stupid shoulder sling under my shirt where no one could even see it.

I remember placing a red-hot car cigarette lighter on the tip of my tongue—you know, the old push-in kind. For some reason, I pushed it in, it popped out, and I paused for an ignorant second before touching my tongue to that fiery coil, just to confirm that it was, in fact, red hot. My sisters were in the car with me, screaming, "What are you doing?" I got ice cream to help with the pain, but it hurt like hell for days. Surprisingly, there was no permanent damage.

I somehow managed to slice my forehead open on a guide wire from a telephone pole and was driven to the emergency room with my head in my mother's lap. I remember my dad trying to skateboard, falling, and breaking his pinky—the same pinky he used to pick his nose with, freely and regularly, while reading the newspaper. It seems appalling now, but back then it was just normal.

There was no parental supervision whatsoever, or at least none that I can remember. I mean none. I don't recall any real rules or restrictions until I was old enough to drive. At a very early age; probably first or second grade, my friends and I climbed over a neighbor's fence and swam in their pool in broad daylight. I didn't know how to swim, so I just watched.

I also tried a cigarette at age six with my friend Tommy-what's-his-name, who had stolen a pack from his dad. I've never gagged and coughed so hard in my life—well, maybe later in college. (An explanation may follow in a later chapter.)

I remember watching the moon landing on TV. I remember watching the nightly news about the Vietnam War. Executions on the street, self-immolation by monks and burned children from napalm. Every night there was a body count of the dead American soldiers. We watched racial violence, race riots, murders and assassinations. All of this we watched on a 19-inch black and white television together as a family. No wonder I was afraid of the dark and insisted on sleeping with the lights on.

And I climbed trees.

I fell out of one from about thirty feet up and somehow walked away with nothing more than the wind knocked out of me. It's occurred to me that tree climbing may be an activity children don't really do anymore. A thing of the past. I wonder why that is. Too dangerous? Not exciting enough?

I was a skilled and daring tree climber and was always looking for new trees to conquer. Sometimes I climbed fifty or even sixty feet if the tree allowed it. There was no fear of heights or danger at that age. The only time

I fell was when a branch broke beneath me.

Tree climbing is a wonderful activity which requires planning, strength, agility, and problem-solving. There's also a quiet, meditative quality to it. At the top, it becomes a beautiful, hidden world, above everything, invisible to the people below. I would spend hours up there, peaceful and completely absorbed. The sounds you hear at the tops of trees are sounds most people have never heard. It is something very special. Sometimes you could even sway with the wind. Magical!

In the winter, I'd make snowballs, climb a tree near the road, and drop them on passing cars. No one ever looked up. Sometimes a driver would stop, furious, get out, and search for the culprit, never thinking to look above them; before eventually driving off, cursing. Probably not the safest or kindest thing to do, but safety wasn't exactly a priority back then.

I once tried to build a treehouse and was somewhat successful. It wasn't very sturdy and I didn't have much help with the design or construction. Eventually, it started to fall apart, and I tore it down because it became unsafe.

I also went through a model-building phase. Back then, we used airplane glue. I built cars and planes, mostly. The process was tedious, and I often got frustrated, ending up with fingers stuck together or parts glued in the wrong place. Sometimes, in a fit of rage, I would smash the entire model and throw it in the trash.

I guess I was never very good at building things like that.

I've since tried doing Legos with my son and have come to hate them just as much as those old models. Model building and Lego sets require patience and the ability to follow instructions.... two things I've never been particularly good at.

Other things I remember about my childhood: moving to Florida at the age of 8. Going to the beach with my family and having the lifeguards call everyone out of the water because of shark sightings, then watching men shoot at the sharks from high towers with high-powered rifles. Seriously, I'm not making that up. It really did happen.

I remember being mean to my neighbor Steven, who had a really bad limp and, for some reason, constantly bit his hand, causing it to be seriously red and irritated. I'm sorry I was mean to you, Steven.

I remember my other neighbor, Phillip Mudd, who was related to the famous news anchor Roger Mudd.

Once, I stepped into a colony of red fire ants. They were all over me in seconds. I ran home screaming bloody murder, and my mother put me in the tub. Ants floating everywhere.

On special occasions, we would go to Venetian Pool, a sort of cross between a lake and a pool, with tunnels you could swim into and diving boards coming out of rock formations. There was an age requirement for jumping off the highest board, but being rather tall for my age, I had no problem. I would spend all day jumping off the high dive. Unfortunately, I would sometimes get a really bad earache from jumping (not diving) off the high dive too many times.

There were hurricanes.

I remember walking to a store by myself (I was 9 years old) to buy really weird items, such as a stuffed parrot or glass balls. Once, on one of these excursions, I saw two people's legs sticking out of a car. One person, the girl; had her legs spread wide, while the other person; the man, had his legs inside the woman's spread legs. They were gyrating and making the car move, and there were moans, maybe screams, I'm not sure. To this day, I wonder if I had witnessed a rape. God, I hope not.

I remember going to the Reptile Gardens, where there were pits of crocodiles and alligators, and hearing rumors of a boy falling into one of the pits and being torn apart and eaten. There were also glass cages where all kinds of poisonous snakes were held, some striking the glass when you tapped on it. One time, the snake handlers brought out a king cobra and milked its venom into a glass jar.

We would sometimes go to some parrot spectacle where parrots were dressed in costumes and would ride unicycles across a little guidewire.

I remember pooping my pants on the bus ride home from school. It was just one of those moments where there was nothing I could have done. I gave it up to the ultimate humiliation. I just rode home, remaining very still, silent, and stinky, dreading my stop, when I would have to take the long walk of shame down the bus aisle, waddling and scooting, trying not to make it obvious or any messier than it already was.

I remember playing stickball and wall ball. Once, while playing wall ball, I fell into an open metal window corner and suffered a very deep cut in my shoulder. I remember looking down at it and seeing yellow. That accident required several stitches.

I also remember stories my father and mother told me about my childhood but which I cannot remember. Once, I was hiking with my dad and his friend Sam, and I fell and busted my chin open. (Does everyone have a scar underneath their chin?) I was taken to the emergency room but would not allow the doctor to put stitches in because I was thrashing and fighting so violently. The doctor asked my father to leave the room. I later told my father that the doctor threatened me with the old "you will never see your father again if you don't let me stitch you up." I don't remember that event at all. Perhaps it was too traumatizing. My dad was so furious he went back to the hospital to "have a talk" with the doctor.

There's also the story of my near drowning. Again, no supervision. My father took me along to visit his rabbi friend, who had a pool in his backyard. They were drinking and smoking and having deep conversations while I made my way around the perimeter of the pool, holding on to the edge. I didn't know how to swim at that time. My father evidently noticed that I was lying at the bottom of the pool. He dove in and pulled me out. I don't remember any of this. I was promptly given swimming lessons after that.

My parents really never pushed me in any way to do anything…..not sports or academics. It seems that, because I was the youngest, I was left on my own. I was free to roam, and I did. I would ride my bike everywhere, many times by myself. There was no limit to where I could go, no boundaries given to me.

Once, while living in Florida, my dad brought me to a tennis club, but he left me out in front of the club, where there was a pond. He gave me a fishing pole and some bait. I couldn't have been much older than 8. Some man came along and told me I couldn't fish there. I don't think he worked for the tennis club, and he was very intimidating to an 8-year-old. I waited around for my dad to finish playing tennis for hours.

My father used to let me ride in our VW Bug, standing up with my head out of the sunroof. I loved it! A policeman pulled us over one time and warned my father that this practice was unsafe. My father got into a little argument with the officer, who quickly threatened to arrest him if he did not comply. He reluctantly capitulated.

How did children survive back then? I was born in 1960, and there were very few laws or common practices for child safety that my family followed. Perhaps they didn't exist. Driving around with your 8-year-old son sticking halfway out of a sunroof must have been the limit.

Once, my dad dropped me off at a pond to ice skate by myself. I was 10 years old. There was no one there but me. No one! Who did that? I could have fallen through the ice. Never heard of child endangerment back then.

We moved a lot. Next to military families, ministers' families are a close second in the "moving around a lot" department. Whatever the reasons for moving, or the jobs my father held, lost, or decided to leave; moving was a regular part of our family life. We usually didn't last too long, two to five years maximum.

Moving around didn't seem to have an immediate effect on me. I didn't seem to mind that much. Too young to care, I guess. It was fun to move to new places, and there were usually a bunch of kids running around in the neighborhoods, so I didn't have much trouble joining in. But, as I said before, I never made any lasting friendships. Another casualty of moving around often.

Moving was fine when I was very young, but when I got older, around eight years old and on—I began to spend more time by myself. I had no need for friends. Moving around may have also contributed to my general negative attitude about staying in one place too long.

I've always felt the need to keep moving, even though I've been stuck in Des Moines for most of my adult life. I tried to escape many times. I was never successful. Des Moines is a lot like heroin. It is addictive, sedative-like.

Moving around a lot has also made me feel unattached, a feeling that has stuck with me to this day. I have no sentimentality, none. I could pick up and move at the drop of a hat. If only we could. Where would we move to? Who am I kidding? I'm way too scared to move now. Way too settled and insecure. Way too full of anxiety. And way too connected to my family's roots.

The roots are not mine by blood; they are by marriage. But they are roots.

My father used to call Des Moines "the asshole of the country," or was it "armpit"? Either way…No one would really choose to live here. It's rather dull, yet safe. No recognizable landforms. Flat farmland with a few cities and suburbs. The people are somewhat nice, conservative, and not overly exciting. Social circles are too small, if you know what I mean.

I always dreamed of living somewhere a little more exciting. Des Moines is definitely not exciting. It's not flashy or cosmopolitan. The weather sucks for the most part. It is unbearably hot and humid in the summer and bitterly cold in the winter. You'd think I'd get used to it, but I haven't.

Here's how the moving around a lot went. I was born in a suburb of Philadelphia called Rosland. When I was two years old, we moved to Fox Hall, Maryland. We must have lived there for about four years. We then moved to Coral Gables, Florida, when I was about six. When I was eight or nine, at the start of my fourth-grade year, we moved to Langhorne, Pennsylvania. Finally, when I was thirteen, going into seventh grade, we moved to Des Moines, Iowa. Probably the hardest move for me.

My father was not always a minister. He started out a Presbyterian minister in Detroit, Michigan, and continued through our move to Rosland. Then he became a lobbyist for the Presbyterian Church in D.C. In Florida, he worked for the Dade County Race Relations Board during the 1960s—a time of great tension, the Civil Rights Movement, and race riots in many major cities. My father was proud of the fact that there had been no race riots in Miami, Florida, during his tenure.

It was during this time that he met and rode in a limousine with Martin Luther King Jr. He told us the story of the ride. Dr. King was very nervous at this point in his life, as his life had been constantly threatened. He knew his days were numbered. At one point during the limousine ride, a car backfired, and Dr. King lurched down to seemingly avoid what he thought was gunfire.

It was one year later that MLK was assassinated on my birthday, April 4th.

My parents were very involved in the Civil Rights Movement. My father, among other things, was elected to the city council in Rosland, Pennsylvania. During this time, he wrote a weekly column in the local newspaper. One such column featured the welcoming of mixed-race married couples into the Presbyterian church at a time when this was not common or acceptable in societal norms. His life was threatened because of this, and he received several hate letters condemning him. He kept a scrapbook of the articles and the hate mail for documentation.

It seems crazy that this was going on while we were a seemingly normal family. Everything seemed just like it should be. Our family was featured in the local paper, with pictures of everyone (everyone but me, as I had not been born) smiling and acting normal. We looked like such a happy family, normal in every sense of the word.

Just a few years earlier, my mother had had a serious nervous breakdown and completely checked out of life. My father requested that her sisters come to Rosland and help, as the house had fallen into ruins, with dirty diapers everywhere and my mother unable to care for her children.

Because I was so much younger than my two sisters, I was much like an only child. I entertained myself quite well, thank you. Exploring was my favorite thing to do; exploring the woods and creeks, and the cityscape on my own.

I created an alter ego for myself that I sometimes thought was God, especially when things didn't go well. Sometimes I got really mad at God and would curse at him, often for the pettiest reasons.

Once while exploring the woods near my home in Langhorne, Pennsylvania I made a strange and disturbing discovery. It was a wooden shed built half below the ground with a door and roof above the ground. I was by myself so I remember feeling very afraid but also curious as to what could be in this shed in the middle of the woods. It was scary, but I decided to open the door and look inside. It squeaked. There was very little light, only the light from the door opening. I looked inside and wasn't sure what was on the floor of the shed. It looked like books or magazines. I got the courage up to jump down inside and as I examined the materials I discovered that it was indeed magazines. Magazines of naked girls and boys doing things. It was a shed full of pornographic magazines. (I realized later in life.) Mounds and mounds of it. I must have been about 10 or 11 years old at the time so I had no idea what this stuff was. Then I got scared. I got really scared and I jumped out of that shed and ran. I ran through the woods to my bike that I left by the road and I rode home as fast as I could. I don't remember much more about this incident other than the dark insidious, and evil feelings it left me with. I never told anyone about it but the implications of it are somewhat disturbing. I mean who builds a shed in the middle of the woods and fills it with pornographic literature? I've had a little experience with pornography in my day but this, this was, and still is disconcerting and bizarre. Who did this? What if they had been there when I stumbled across it? I consider myself very lucky.

The Art of Body Surfing

"You can't stop the waves but you can learn to surf."
-Jon Kabat-Zinn

I sit and contemplate the infinite possibilities of things going wrong in my/our life. I wake up with a sinking, uncertain feeling. It is out of my control, but I am wrestling with it. I am not winning, but I am kind of holding my own. It doesn't matter what I'm worried about, in fact, there are no specifics. It is all-encompassing, far-reaching, and comes upon me in huge waves. Unrelenting waves of anxiety and panic crashing upon the shores of my consciousness. How's that for a metaphor? And a segue.

I used to love the ocean. I fell in love with it when I was a young boy. My family vacationed at the beach every summer, usually Rehoboth Beach or Dewey Beach. I learned how to swim in the waves and taught myself how to body surf. There is a certain art to body surfing; a timing that is hard to explain. You learn how to feel the backward pull of the wave and then the surge forward. If you know this magical moment, you catch the wave and ride it like a human surfboard.

Body surfing, for me, was a connection to something so huge and awesome that it became euphoric. It was losing myself. I had no fear. It wasn't until I became an adult that I developed a little fear of the ocean. The ocean will chew you up and spit you out. It will take you down where you will never be found, down into the infinite. It has no conscience, no remorse, no prejudices, and no guilt. That's what I love about it.

Trying to explain how to body surf to someone is difficult. I've tried a few times, but I usually end up saying, "you just have to feel it." Body surfing takes some practice, and some serious wipeouts will most likely occur. I lost a little skin and gained some scrapes and soreness while learning. Even as a child and teenager, I would wake up the next morning feeling like I had been in an eight-hour wrestling match, and lost.

Getting too far out in front of a wave was dangerous because it could slam you headfirst into the ocean floor. I learned to put my arms out in front and roll if this ever happened. Sometimes I would do this on purpose because it was such a rush to flip and be tossed about in the crashing wave.

Catching large waves was the most exciting and the most fun. It could also be dangerous if it was the wrong kind of wave. Large waves that have no gradual building or roll are not good waves for body surfing. They crash quickly and hard and usually smash you down violently. I learned this the hard way, of course.

Knowing that you've caught the perfect wave just right and riding and gliding within it is a one-of-a-kind experience. If you're lucky, at the end of the ride you get caught up in the white water and churned all about as the wave is crashing, disappearing into the wave and finally emerging out of the mass as the wave loses its energy.

Oh yeah! Nothing like it. Nothing like it at all.

One of my favorite things to do in the ocean was to float in the area where the waves crashed and just get pummeled by the breaking waves. Spinning and being tossed around like a rag doll, I would laugh out loud under the water, exalted, as if I was toying with one of the most powerful things on earth. My brother-in-law at the time, Doug, taught me this, and I am forever grateful for it. Onlookers would stop and look at me with dismay and confusion as to what the hell I was doing, washing up at their feet laughing and spitting, then running and diving back in for more.

I met Doug when my sister Andrea brought him home to meet our family. I was about ten years old at the time. He immediately took a great interest in me, and he proved to be a profound influence on my life throughout the relatively short time he was married to my sister.

There was a very close connection that I felt to him. He was also amazingly sarcastic and funny and brutally honest. He got me, and I loved him dearly. It was like having a big brother, but a kind and caring big brother. He was an adult who never wanted to grow up—a kid at heart.

For Christmas one year, I received this really cool hockey game with sliding players that you controlled by pulling, pushing, and turning rods. You could pass to your own players, and you had a goalie that you could defend with—kind of like foosball, if you've ever played that. He and I played that game for hours upon hours.

He really became a part of our family, especially after they were married. He took me to my first baseball game at Yankee Stadium. He smoked, which was cool back then. He played with me and talked with me, and he made everyone laugh.

He would come on vacations with us to the shore. We would play paddleball on the beach, which was fun when played normally, but we played it differently, hitting the ball way up in the air to each other—kind of like paddle balling high fly balls back and forth. We did not have complete control over where the ball would go, so we would end up running up and down the beach, looking up in the air and rushing to whack the ball back up into the air for each other to hit before it touched the ground. We must have looked incredibly strange and would occasionally get carried away and run across some stranger's towels. I'm sure we pissed off a few people. But we became really good at it after an hour, and it was really fun.

We would also play cribbage for hours on end with my two sisters. We routinely went to movies at least once during our vacation at the shore. I remember seeing *The Sting* with Paul Newman and Robert Redford and thinking that was pretty good. We also saw *Blazing Saddles*, which none of us thought was very funny, and we all walked out.

One night, we went to see *Jaws*. Not a great movie to see while vacationing at the shore. But Doug was like, "this is bullshit," and after the movie was over, he insisted we all go down to the beach and go swimming at night. We were all too afraid, but Doug went in and swam with no fear (I think), and we all stood on the shore pleading with him to come out of the water at once.

As I got older, I began to see girls on the beach during our vacations. I mean, I became aware of girls. One year, at the age of 16, I had my eye on this one girl that I thought was just beautiful. We would see her every day by herself. Doug and my sister would encourage me to go talk to her.

I was very shy and had no nerve for it, but one day she was coming down with her things, and I got up the nerve to ask her if I could help put up her umbrella. As it so happens, on this day I also, embarrassingly enough, decided to wear a European bathing suit. You know, the man bikini? Let's just say I was experimenting, and failing.... with looking cool.

I felt super uncomfortable in this man bikini, and it was something I had never done before and would never do again. I also had no idea how to put up an umbrella on the beach, but I decided it would be a way to talk to this beautiful girl.

So, as I'm trying to be cool, I accidentally break her beach umbrella. I mean, I hear it crack and see that I have severely damaged it because I don't know how to put it in the sand properly. So, I just sort of apologized and walked away in my man bikini.

It was an extremely humiliating experience.

The next year at the shore, I met these two girls and a guy, and we kind of hung out a little bit. I was, of course, attracted to both girls and was very interested in, and frightened of having sex with one of them. The guy was not involved with either girl, so it seemed like the odds were in my favor.

I was able to drive at the time, but being only 16, I could not drive on my own. Well, it just so happened that there was a Peter Frampton concert taking place about an hour and a half away in Ocean City, and I kind of told these kids that I could drive us all down there to see the show. Of course, I knew that my parents wouldn't let me take their car.

My older sister Jenna had just bought her first new car, a blue Opel Kadett. It was a sweet two-door sports car to me at the time. I began to hatch a plan.

The night of the concert, my family was planning to go out to dinner and see a movie. I asked if I could hang out with my new friends instead. For some reason, I thought there would be enough time to drive down to Ocean City (52 miles away), see the concert, and drive back before the family got home.

I waited until the family was gone, grabbed the keys to my sister's Opel Kadett, and we were off to Ocean City. It was kind of a scary ride. I remember not being that great of a driver, especially at night. On occasion, I would go off the road onto the grass median between the lanes, at one point almost wiping out.

Of course, there were no tickets available when we got there, so we hung out for a little bit and drove back. As it turned out, my family decided not to go to the movies, so when I drove up in my sister's new Opel Kadett, the whole family was waiting for me. My sister Jenna was extremely pissed off.

It was a sour end to that year's vacation at the shore. Needless to say, my endeavors with the girls did not work out, and I ended up writing my sister a long apology letter when I got back to Iowa.

Many years later, while in my late twenties, I went into the ocean on a rather cloudy, somewhat stormy day. The waves were rough, and I probably shouldn't have been out there. As I was walking back into shore, I stepped on something that felt like a broken bottle. I knew for sure that I was bleeding and got out of the water as fast as I could.

When I got up to shore and lay down to see what had happened, the pain began to intensify. There was a small puncture on the top of my foot, gushing blood. I figured out that I had just stepped on a stingray. My sister Andrea was there with me, and she rushed me home.

The pain was unbearable as the venom spread throughout my leg. It felt as though my entire leg was being roasted on a fire. I was writhing in agony. My sister and my wife at the time took me to urgent care, where they gave me a shot of Thorazine and pulled the barbs out of my foot. I flew home in a wheelchair.

My comfort in the ocean changed after that experience. I became a little less carefree and a little more careful. But the ocean still calls me back, and I swim and body surf in her whenever I can.

Incidentally, the word "thalassophile" means a lover of the sea, someone who loves the ocean. I'm proud to call myself a thalassophile. A very cautious one.

The Game of Life

"The game of life is a game of boomerangs. Our thoughts, deeds and words return to us sooner or later with astounding accuracy."
-Florence Scovel Shinh

I am afraid of the drugs that I have been prescribed for anxiety and depression. But I am afraid of just about everything these days. I know I should take them, but I don't. This is a symptom of severe anxiety and depression. You don't have the time or the patience to wait for the drugs to work, so you don't take them.

It's a terrible thing to live your life in fear. Most normal people experience fear in short bursts or under certain circumstances. Imagine a time when you were deathly afraid, an experience that made you feel incredibly vulnerable, like failure, rejection, the death of a loved one, extreme uncertainty, panic or running for your life from a pack of hyenas. When you have severe anxiety, this is how you feel every moment of every hour of every day. It is ultimately what breaks you. Fear of everything. It takes a toll.

Occasionally, I will experience glimpses of myself or forget about the "unbearable," but then the anxiety and fear of the unknown and the uncertain will creep back in, and I will have intense panic attacks. How is it possible that one year ago I was so different? One year ago, I lived in the present. Yes, I was a bit obsessive and prone to anxiety. I tended to worry and be overly concerned about our son's well-being and money, but I was at least present.

Now, sometimes I can actually feel separate from myself. I know that sounds strange. In fact, spell check is wanting me to combine the words "my" and "self" into "myself," but I won't do it. It is as though I am an automaton doing a task, yet I am floating away nearby, observing and freaking out.

I never thought it would come to this. But I apparently have lost the ability to trust and have faith. As humans, we have to live with a certain degree of trust and blind faith. We must bury our heads in the sand and get on with life because, if we really looked around and took in what's going on around us, we would be scared shitless.

The ultimate trick to living, as I said before, is distraction. You have to distract yourself from the pain and suffering in the world and the inevitable doom with tasks, duties, and entertainment. I have lost the art of distraction. Distractions just give me more anxiety. Life consumes me. I have to relearn how to play the game of life. If you don't play along, you find yourself doubting and fearful.

I've forgotten how to play. It's like I am in perpetual limbo, neither living nor dying, just here getting through the day.

As the outlaw Josey Wales once said, "it's time to get busy living or get busy dying." As it turns out, that line was used again in *The Shawshank*

Redemption. I've got to get busy living.

The Demise of Education, the World and Me

"Only two things are infinite, the universe and human stupidity, and I'm not sure about the former.
-Albert Einstein

According to the National Literary Institute, 21% of adults in the US are illiterate, 54% of adults have literacy below a 6th-grade level, and 130 million adults are now unable to read a simple story to their children. Those numbers might be a little generous, in my opinion. And from my experience in the classroom, I can guarantee you that the writing skills of Americans are even worse.

These statistics should be frightening to everyone, but most people are probably not aware of them because they are too occupied with their own lives, or they're too stupid. Ironic, huh?

I became a teacher rather late in life. I was in my thirties, recently divorced, with a six-year-old daughter. My daughter was one of my main inspirations for becoming a teacher. I loved to read with her and was fascinated with her ability to learn. I decided that being a teacher was a way to hopefully make some kind of positive contribution to the world by serving others and making a difference in my community. To me, being an educator was a calling, if you will. It was what I thought to be a valuable and worthy profession.

I quit my job in health insurance and got a job at my local middle school as a special education teacher associate. This was my day job, and at night I went to education classes at an off-site university program. I learned from actual teachers, not from professors who hadn't been in the classroom for decades. I enjoyed my classes and was excited about getting my first job and my first classroom.

The last twelve weeks of my teacher education program were spent student teaching, six weeks in a first-grade class and six weeks in a fifth-grade class. I had no idea how I was going to make this work, as I could not work full time and do my student teaching, but I kept on going, somehow having faith that I would find a way.

It just so happened that I had a rich aunt die and leave me some money at the perfect time to finance my student teaching. This was an amazing, unbelievable coincidence that I did not realize the gravity of until much later. A random leap of faith on my part and a well-timed miracle that allowed me to become a teacher.

I was not glad that my aunt died, even though she was suffering from Alzheimer's disease, but it would seem that I was destined to become a teacher. Not sure that was a good thing or a bad thing after all was said and done. Yet another fork in the road. Random ambiguity strikes again!

It was a difficult and challenging twelve weeks of experiencing first-hand what it was like to be a teacher. When I finished my degree, I got a long-term special education substitute position at my old school. I then taught another year in special education but decided that was not for me.

My first year of "real teaching" was at an elementary school teaching fifth grade. I co-taught with a teacher who was retiring after that year and, quite frankly, was just trying to make it through her last year. She was a horrible teacher, in my opinion.

I taught my group of kids in the morning, which was fine, and then I got her group of students in the afternoon. They were a completely different group, very disrespectful and very unmotivated. My co-teacher, who had them in the morning, gave them no consequences, did not want parent involvement, and yelled at them most of the time.

I barely made it through that first year. A student got up in my face and threatened to "punch me in the mouth." I almost quit several times, and probably should have.

The following year, I got my dream job of teaching sixth-grade Social Studies at the middle school where I had worked before as a teacher associate. Things were pretty much great for the next 16 years.

The students were wonderful most of the time. They were fun, motivated, smart, creative, and, for the most part, respectful. I loved teaching most of the time. There were some bad years and some really good years, but I was always hopeful and always felt that my job was rewarding. Students were learning, and I made learning interesting and fun.

It was during the last three years of teaching that things began to deteriorate.

During the last few years of my career, the school boundaries changed, and so did the demographics. The majority of students were now middle class, impoverished, and children of refugees from mostly African countries. There were still some old-wealth students at the school, but those kids were bussed to an off-site campus to attend higher-level courses. This left very few kids who could model learning and many kids who were dealing with broken families, mental health issues, and who knows what that went on in the government housing projects.

Many of the students from African countries were illiterate in their own language. I remember having two girls in for a lunch detention who lived in the projects, and they were quite honest with me about how scary it was to live there. These girls would be really great students one day, sweet and participating in classroom activities. But the next day they would turn into holy hell, bat-shit crazy. They could be very lovely, and they could be very mean and confrontational.

I distinctly remember them telling me that "you don't want to know what goes on in our neighborhood." The entire school got free lunch because over 80% of the students were below the poverty line.

It was during the last three years of teaching that I began to grow increasingly anxious. It was a steady decline. Each year worse than the last. The next-to-last year of my teaching, students were so bad that I began to experience post-traumatic stress–related symptoms.

On a daily basis, students were out of control, with horrible behavior and rampant disrespect. It wasn't normal middle school behavior, it was full-blown mental disorders and verbal attacks from students that made no sense to me. There was little learning and teaching and an enormous amount of conflict, just daily, intense conflict.

Students were mostly working at a low level of reading, writing, and thinking. Administration was not helping with behavior issues, as they were overwhelmed and unwilling to do what was necessary. Every day, I left the building severely traumatized and beaten down.

Being totally ignored by students is probably one of the worst forms of disrespect. Sixth-grade girls are especially good at this. Asking them to please be quiet so the rest of the class can learn, asking them to please get off their phones during class, asking them to please not use the word "fuck" in my classroom—which happened on an hourly basis during the last few years—they just ignore you like you're not even there.

Many of the students appeared to me to be so angry at the world that I could feel their hatred the minute they walked into the classroom. Children began to resent being asked to complete a task, follow the simplest of guidelines, or simply read a small passage. Children could not follow directions, even though you had modeled them and shown examples.

Trying to do self-directed projects became a struggle, as kids would abuse computer privileges—exploring inappropriate sites, playing games, or even emailing other students' inappropriate content. I noticed a severe loss of curiosity that was replaced by students simply "Googling" specific questions and accepting the information that was given. Teaching students to use trusted sources of information was extremely difficult because they wanted instant answers.

It was the lack of interest in learning that got to me the most. Having to motivate the severely unmotivated every single minute of every single day is just exhausting—and boring, I might add. I guess I just found the students petty, tedious, immature, and uninspiring.

Add to this mixture a great majority of children in each class who were in such need of therapy, love, and attention that it seemed like an impossible, hopeless task. The last thing these kids were looking for was an education.

They had been beaten down into thinking that they could not change their circumstances or their future. We began to teach them to think that they could control their future and that education was the key.

It didn't work.

For me, ultimately, the emotional drain and daily trauma became too much. They wore me down to the point where I would simply put my feet up on the desk and wait for them to notice that I was waiting for them.

I tried many tricks over the last few years. Playing my guitar worked for a little while. Clapping a rhythm that required a response was our school-wide attention grabber. It's just that when you have to do this 5–10 times a class period, it gets old for both students and teachers. In some classrooms, it was a total bust most days. I mean, a complete waste of time. There was nothing I could do but survive the hour.

When a student's hand went up, it was usually to ask, "When is this class over?" (The schedule was posted in eight different areas around the room, and we had been in class for over half the year.) On my darkest, most hopeless days, I would respond, "Not soon enough." Then, as the bell rang for students to go, I would say, "Please leave," and they thought I was being rude. Ha!

As I left the room on a daily basis, I would raise my arms in triumph and say under my breath, "I survived!" Sometimes I said it too loudly.

I had some classrooms where students would literally chase each other around the room and roll around on the floor. Yeah, I could go on, but you get the picture. I don't do well in chaos. I need structure and a modicum of control. I equated every day with going to war—traumatized from going into battle every day and fighting a losing, hopeless war.

The strange thing is, some of these students would say things to me in private, such as "you're my favorite teacher" or "this is my favorite class." I wanted to say, "Then why in the hell don't you act like it?" That's the most amazing thing—the students had no idea that what they were doing was incredibly rude, disrespectful, and just downright mean.

Mind you, this is "little ole" Des Moines now, not some big-city inner-city school.

I would lay awake at night trying to figure out how to reach kids, asking myself, "What is wrong with me?" "I am a terrible teacher." I began to be afraid—afraid of what the students would do, afraid that my class set of computers would not be charged, afraid that my principal or some other administrator would come to my classroom and witness this hell and judge me for being a terrible teacher.

The thing is, I used to think I was a pretty good teacher. I designed projects and fun group competitions. Students were creating videos, murals, performing music, competing against each other by presenting projects to the class. They did this on their own for the most part. Some needed a little more of a push than others, but it was not a full-time job trying to motivate them. Once they were given the bait, they went after it. That, to me, is good teaching—staying out of students' way and letting them find their avenue of interest within the framework given.

Some kids would come up with their own ideas, and I was elated. It was inspiring. Some days the class would be so into their work that I would ask them if they needed me for anything. They would reply, "No, Mr. S., we're good." It was fun! They had fun too. It was also learning. It gave me chills on a regular basis.

There was book work, and homework, and yes, tests. Kids were motivated to do well. But something changed in the last few years. I wasn't as funny as I used to be. Kids thought of me as just plain old, I think. And I lost trust in them. I no longer liked or respected them very much, and they could probably sense that.

They were just not as bright, creative, curious, or motivated to work. My projects that offered choice usually meant they did nothing unless I was on top of them all the time. Even then, they did very little, and what they did was, quite frankly, shit. Just getting directions out to the class became difficult. Students' abilities were so low that scaffolding materials became necessary, and spoon-feeding was necessary for everyone. Even brighter students were not interested or motivated.

Soon, a new grading system was implemented to help students pass: Standard Reference Grading. This was basically a way of dumbing down everything so students could do as little as possible and still pass, while at the same time not motivating brighter students to excel. It seemed wrong to me. It became almost dishonest. A dirty, big, fat, smelly lie. A cover-up to make the schools look better than they really were.

This really hit home when administrators began to tell us what to say and what not to say at parent conferences. We were not to talk about poor behavior. We were trained often in various ways to deal with conflicts. The data at our school showed fewer office behavior referrals, but that was because we were looked down upon for sending kids to the office, so we just sucked it up and dealt with kids cursing all the time, multiple disruptions, and downright rude, disrespectful behavior on a major level.

We would all smirk at these meetings that showed how awesome we were doing. Many of us asked, "Then why do I leave this place feeling so awful every day?" Teachers would meet with union representatives and break down and sob at how dangerous the school was and how kids treated them.

Students were out of control in the hallways and would not take directions. They were constantly late to classes. At one point, I went in to talk with the vice principal about how dangerous the out-of-control hallways were, and he basically told me there was nothing he could do.

The students who cause the most problems have no parents who have control over their own kids. Children behave in the manner in which they were raised. They are a product of their home life. Kids were no longer held accountable either by the school or their parents.

The bar was lowered for everyone, and they all rejoiced.

And the pot of water with the frog was placed on the burner.

And the burner was lit.

My last year of teaching was one of the darkest times of my life. I was experiencing night sweats from anxiety, and that was when I could sleep. I would wake up, take a shower, and curl up in a ball on the floor in the spare bedroom, writhing in anxiety, not wanting to go to school.

I would walk around, flailing my arms in convulsing, moaning rhythms. I was in full-blown severe anxiety mode, living in terror every day. I barely survived on anti-anxiety medication and was hospitalized for seriously thinking about suicide.

My anxiety took hold and became a part of me.

During this last year, I knew what to expect the minute I arrived in my classroom. It was one incident after another, depending on which students were there.

My first period had these four girls from Liberia who were just plain mean and confrontational. They would laugh and speak in their native language, carrying on conversations across the room and ignoring any of my requests to stop. Eventually, they would ignore their assigned seats and sit next to each other, challenging me to request that they move back to their assigned seats. Meanwhile, other classmates would follow their lead and move around, ignore requests, and so on.

I was not above yelling from time to time, but that was not my way of dealing with poor behavior. Every day was the same—these girls would either disrupt the class, refuse to comply, or be sent out of the room.

At the same time, there was also a boy in this class who either bounced off the walls or slept. There were other boys and girls who were clearly going through an attraction ritual, and two other girls who seemed to be very depressed.

Attendance and tardiness were constant issues, and everyone was at least two grade levels below reading level and perhaps four grade levels below in academic performance, critical thinking, and maturity. I had a special education teacher who came in every other day but often missed her day with me because she hated it as much as I did.

In every class period, there were several serious incidents, several confrontations, which left me anxious and traumatized. I would hope for certain students to be gone. I would send some students to the office, but they would be back in the classroom in minutes.

I would help the students who wanted help, but the behavior of other students took up most of my time. The look in the eyes of the students who wanted to learn was heartbreaking.

My fourth period was probably the worst. It was after lunch, so I had to somehow get them to follow me back from the insane lunchroom to our class, where the insanity would continue.

This class was full of students with severe problems, including a lesbian cutter who was struggling with her identity, two boys from the government housing project who—I don't even know where to begin to describe—their hatred of their mothers and general overall misogynistic indecencies. There was another rather large boy who was just plain crazy and completely incapable of doing anything academic. He would often roll around on the floor or on top of tables.

This class took a good 20 minutes to get started and then was full of constant blowups, disruptions, refusals to follow directions, and inappropriate behaviors that would leave me, again, filled with trauma and severe anxiety.

This, along with whatever horrors you might encounter in the hallways, happened on a daily basis—every day, without fail—to the point of me finally losing it.

It was November of 2017, shortly before Thanksgiving, that I finally succumbed to PTSD and severe anxiety and went on medical leave. I was out for 12 weeks, and although I was not in the school situation, I was still living with severe anxiety and depression.

I went back to work just after spring break and hung on until the end of the school year. I was unable to return to teaching and, in turn, was left with crippling anxiety. I retired early with a partial pension.

It was not a happy retirement. There was nothing to celebrate. It was not even really a retirement. It was an abandon-ship, save-yourself leaving of a career that has taken just about everything from me.

My experience as a teacher has left me with more than personal anxiety but also anxiety about the condition of our public schools, our teacher's health, the children who attend, and the adults that they will become. My anxiety doesn't let me live in a comfortable little corner of the world; this is too small of an area for my anxiety to play with. My anxiety forces me to consider "everything," especially in what I perceive to be the world's slow decay into idiocrasy. The most insidious fact about this decay is that it is happening right under our collective noses. Most of the people of this country are either too stupid or too caught up in their own lives to notice this demise. Carl Sagan writes, …" The dumbing down of America is most evident in the slow decay of substantive content in the enormously influential media, the 30-second sound bites (now down to 10 seconds or less), lowest common denominator programming, credulous presentations on pseudoscience and superstition, but especially a kind of celebration of ignorance." In my opinion the root of this "dumbing down" is the lack of critical thinking, quality education, and finally social media.

The education system of today is severely outdated and is in great need of repair. Today's students are faltering in intelligence, integrity, curiosity, critical thinking, thought-sustaining ability, problem-solving, as well as reading, writing, and math skills. The notion of hard work has been lost and replaced with instant gratification. If it's not easy to find or do, then why bother? If it requires detail and investigation, they get bored. Students are confusing the notion of hard work with boredom.

All of this is the result of increasing poverty and mental illness and, to a great degree, the onslaught of social media. Children today are exposed to things that we were never exposed to. They are learning things not from their parents or even friends, but from the internet. And the internet has no filter.

Their brains are not able to process the information they receive via social media about sex, relationships, politics, dishonesty, morals, truth, integrity, and so much more, to the point that they think what they see on the internet is normal behavior and all is true. This brain drain is not unique to children—it's also happening to adults as well.

According to teacher-turned cognitive neuroscientist Jared Cooney Horvath, "Generation Z (Gen Z) has been identified as the first generation in modern history to show lower cognitive abilities—specifically in memory, attention, and IQ—compared to their parents." The reason for the decline is largely attributed to "increased screen time, reduced reading, and over-reliance on digital technology."

What is really frightening is that, in most cases, "the decline in performance doesn't result in better strategies" ...and that standardized testing has been adjusted to accommodate lower expectations and shorter attention spans. In other words, the education system is not raising the bar for this generation but rather lowering it."

Ever seen the movie *Idiocracy*?

Frankly, our education system needs a complete overhaul. The reliance on technology needs to be tempered. Intense help is needed at early ages, not only with the basic skills of reading, writing, and math, but also with mental health, nutrition, healthy lifestyle training, sustaining effort, mentoring, positive experiences, and family support.

Middle and high school need to be more elective-based, with options for skill-based training and connections to employers and employer training programs. School needs to be shorter. Academics can be accomplished in 3–4 hours, and the rest of the day can focus on home skills, financial literacy, food and nutrition, exercise and health, including a wide variety of sports and activities; arts, dance, music, community projects, and, of course, mental health, group therapy, and counseling.

You may not be aware of this, but the arts are slowly being taken away in many school districts. One of the most important skills not taught in our school systems, but being taught in some European countries, is the ability to discern fact from fiction. Critical thinking must also be taught.

All of this overhaul would require a substantial investment in teachers, staff, and students. Competitive salaries are needed to attract well-trained and qualified people, and to acquire equipment and technology for a school system worthy of today's students.

The likelihood of all of this happening is highly unlikely. For some reason, those in power aren't interested in investing in our children. They don't think our children's education is worth the price.

Think of all the many societal problems that could potentially be erased if education were moved to the forefront of society.

Sadly, education has become a pawn used by political groups to represent evil liberalism, which in turn has resulted in the privatization of schools. Instead, we have book banning and the teaching of white-friendly, guilt-free history.

Those who can afford private schools will receive an education less regulated by the state, while those who attend public schools will suffer. If I didn't know better, it almost seems as if our politicians have hatched an evil plan to keep the masses dumb so that they can control them.

I believe this dysfunctional education system will eventually (has already) lead to an absurd and ridiculous adult population who will blindly follow anyone who appeals to the crap they watch on social media and other outlets of misinformation. Idiocy will become normal and acceptable. It's happening subtly and slowly.

This decay will also cause even greater segregation and resentment between rich and poor, and the educated and the not so educated. Having experienced the rise in the number of students affected by poverty, mental illness, and neglect in my little middle school in Des Moines has made me very afraid for all of us. My anxiety rages on.

Can you imagine what it's like in big cities? Who in their right mind would want to become a teacher in an inner-city school? Or, more importantly, how long can a teacher last in an environment of constant confrontation? It takes it out of you, no matter how strong you are. Battle fatigue.

How do you educate students who are so consumed by social media and media in general that they have lost the ability to read, learn, create, and think on their own?

But, isn't our education system an indictment of society and the overall health of our communities, families, and relations with others? How involved are you with your child's education and school? Let's face it, community and neighborhood schools are becoming a thing of the past. How much information does your child tell you about their day at school? "Guess what Mom? Today Johnny told Mr. S. to suck his dick." How many kids come home and tell their parents that there is very little learning going on in class, because the kids are out of control. Most kids accept and are used to this type of environment so they don't even wonder what the alternative could be. Some kids and parents notice, but most of these students are placed in accelerated classes where learning is at a higher level and student behavior is better. Herein lies the problem of segregation of students from those who are usually from a steady home and have learned the skills needed to achieve at a higher level and those who have none of that, which is the majority of students. Increasingly, wealthier and more educated people insulate themselves from this pariah of decay by moving out into the suburbs and the countryside or in gated communities. While they are not immune to the effects social media has on their children, they can protect themselves with high property taxes, good schools and gates to keep out the plague and plight of inner-city public education. My wife and I are guilty of this to some degree. We moved to the suburbs to find better schools for our son. Who doesn't want the best education for their children? We both were teachers at inner city schools and did not want our son to attend them for many reasons. Our son went to school at a public Montessori school through 6th grade and was sheltered from the horrors of public schools. This school is a secret school known to very few families but well known to many teachers in the Des Moines school district. We put our name on the list to get in before our son was born, and he was admitted there at pre-school age. We loved that school, not so much for academic value, but for the kindness and caring community that was created there. Peace was the motto. It was not forced upon them but introduced and nurtured throughout the school. After Montessori School, our son would have attended schools in an old wealthy and upper middle-class section of Des Moines. These schools are steeped in history and the people that live there are mostly second-generation loyalists to the schools that they themselves attended. They feel a connection to that community which I admire to some degree. Many of their children are in a gifted and talented program of the public-school system and therefore attend a separate central campus school where they can receive a higher level of instruction. They are able to avoid the mainstream public education and the hell that goes on in those classrooms. By the same token this brain segregation brings down the academics in the regular classroom because there are very few to no models of higher thinking.

Our son would not have qualified for the gifted and talented program and would have been thrown to the wolves, so we left. I also have to admit that I feel no real connection to any community. I have no consistent history with the one here, even though I've lived in this city for most of my life.

We believed that, at its worst, the suburban schools would still be better than any inner-city school. Yes, we feel a little guilty about that, but not enough to lose sleep over it.

Interestingly, it was our son who ultimately made the decision. After attending a one-day in-school tour at the suburban middle school near our home, he loved it. He wanted to go there. We're fairly certain we had very little to do with that choice, as we never once revealed our plans about moving school districts.

While I would occasionally share some of my more extreme classroom experiences with him, I don't think that influenced his decision much either.

I see much of what's on social media, mainstream television, and similar outlets as unreal, not normal, but absurd. And yet, many adults are just as entertained and consumed by it as their kids. It's a sick form of entertainment, one that blurs the line between reality and behavioral dysfunction.

We take pleasure in the idiocy of the fools who fill the cyber world, drawn in like moths to a flame. And before you know it, you've been watching for hours.

There's a sense of doom that comes with our ability to access almost anything on the internet instantly; algorithms from hell, designed for mass consumption by the illiterate. It's overwhelming, to the point of hopelessness. There is, of course, no stopping it, and in some ways, we eventually get what we deserve.

Another frog in the pot. The burner is on. The water is getting warmer. And by the time it's boiling, it's too late.

This is the kind of thing I worry about, not in a constructive way, but in a spiraling, anxiety-driven way, every day. I could easily become consumed by the broader decay of society, but now it feels more personal. The anxiety has turned inward. It paralyzes me.

I've retired. I'm done with the trauma of the classroom. But the anxiety is still here.

I just want to know that things are somehow going to be okay.

I used to believe that. I had a saying I leaned on: "Everything will turn out just like it's supposed to." But that doesn't work for me anymore.

Sometimes the "unbearable" becomes so overwhelming that I want it to end.

You know…. end it.

My therapist tells me that anxiety is what drives people to hurt themselves, to kill themselves.

He's right.

Parenting and Children

"I like children, as long as they're properly cooked."
-W.C. Fields

All of my history, my meetings with people, the choices made, the forks in the road taken; have come together to create my children, my family, and the life I have now. Had any one of those intangibles been different… well, you know: random ambiguity.

Being a parent is the hardest damn thing in the world, at least for me. And honestly, it should be that hard for everyone. If it isn't, in my opinion, something is seriously wrong with you, and maybe you shouldn't have had children in the first place.

I even think anyone who wants to have children should have to get a license first. Just basic requirements: over 18, pass a psychological exam, have a job, a steady place to live, no drug or alcohol addictions. That's it. You need a license to drive a car, get married, be a teacher, lawyer, doctor, or nurse—so why not to have a child? It's such a huge decision, such an immense responsibility, affecting not only your life and your child's, but everyone who comes in contact with them.

Maybe reverse-sterilize all males at 15, and only after approval do you get your license to have kids. I'm kidding, of course… right? Pretty sure I wouldn't have passed that psychological exam anyway.

I mean, who in their right mind would logically decide to have children? "Hey honey, let's create a human being that will wake us up at least three times a night to eat or be changed, destroying our sleep habits forever. Let's also clean up its poop, vomit, and drool in no particular order, never knowing the sanctity of privacy again. Oh, and let's ruin the environment with disposable diapers for 2–4 years because cloth diapers were just plain nasty and almost as bad for the planet.

Let's watch them cry as though in agonizing pain, never really knowing what to do and feeling helpless. Then, at six months, let's drop this little human off with a complete stranger, leave them crying hysterically, rip our hearts out, and drown in guilt, all so we can go to work to pay for the care that stranger is giving.

Oh, and let's endlessly worry whether they'll survive those first few years because they get fucking sick all the fucking time with really horrible illnesses that sound like death. Yes, let's give them all sorts of medicine to help them sleep through a cough that keeps everyone up all night. And I only wish they'd get really sick so we could rush them to the emergency room and watch them climb the walls on steroids like a tiny rabid animal.

Then let's put them in preschool, where they'll learn to socialize with children who may or may not be "normal" and pick up strange; and sometimes bad, habits. Can we please always wonder whether we're messing them up and whether we're doing the right thing? Yes! More guilt, please.

And finally, let's know and feel what unconditional love is.

There are in fact, many reasons why people choose to have children, according to various sources here are the top five; Number one is to experience unconditional love, number two is to build a family and create a legacy, number three is to find purpose and meaning, number four is to experience the joy of parenting, and number five is personal growth. Okay, did you notice that for all those reasons, all five of them are purely selfish?

I've heard from several people that they chose to have children because they think that it gives them some sort of immortality and that they will live on forever somehow in their children. Oh, please God no! Please don't let me live on in my children. I hope to be the last of my kind. I hope my children are nothing like me.

For me, being a parent means that your life is never your own, it is split between your children and yourself. You're all in pieces, vexed and never able to fully relax and say, "they'll be alright." I am too conscious, too worrisome, too consumed by their well-being, too doting, too self-evaluating, too selfish, and too afraid that I gave them all sorts of bad genes. I remember the day my wife and I left the hospital after the birth of our son. I've never felt so abandoned and alone in my life. I looked back at the healthcare workers in sheer terror saying, "you mean were on our own? Really?" I mean life is hard and I don't want my children to be hurt by the cruelty of this world. Knowing the horrible things that await your child is heartbreaking. There is no way that you can protect them from all the evil out there. The ultimate fear I think, the ultimate fear for every parent is the fear that something you love more than anything else in the world could be taken away from you at any moment.

Being a parent meant I had to grow up and be an adult, something I never really wanted or cared to do. Adulthood is seriously overrated. For me, parenting meant I had to excel at things I'm terrible at, like being a role model. I'm a horrible role model. I don't brush my teeth regularly, I am habitually late, I hate getting up in the morning and going to bed at night. I have never been optimistic, positive, or particularly smiley. I hate routine, responsibility, ownership, consumerism, and conformity. I despise institutions.

These are not exactly the values or lack of values that make for good parenting in today's world. Forgive me, children.

I am never far from worry with my two children. Being a parent may feel like a blessing to most people, but not to me. While I love both my children to the point of extreme emotional pain, I believe it was not in my best mental health interest to have had them.

My father had this story he told about his days as a young father. Hilarious to some honest listeners, horrifying to others. He told us three children that there were nights when he came in to try to comfort us babies for the third time or so. He was so tired and frustrated that he wanted to "pick us up by the ankles and throw us against the wall." I have felt that way as a young father. I have thought terrible things.

I am ashamed to admit it, but when you are sleepless for so long that you are near crazy, you start thinking things that are not good. I spent many sleepless nights outside, drinking vodka and smoking cigarettes, things I had given up years before my son was born, while he was sick, which was often. I wanted to know why he got sick so much. It drove me to near insanity. Everyone said it was normal, but I could not accept that. It was something I couldn't control, something beyond my control that I desperately needed to control. It drove me to the brink.

I have two parental experiences: one with my daughter, which was mostly long-distance parenting at best, and a more recent one with my son, whom we have raised from birth. My most recent parental journey began at Callanan Middle School, where I spent 20 years teaching and where I met my wife. We were friends at first, going for walks with our dogs and spending time together. When we became a couple, we had to hide it from both the students and the staff. I was fifteen and a half years older than her, but we decided that was not a barrier to our life together. After two years, we had a beautiful son, and those first few years of parenthood were some of the most difficult days of my life. Parenting has been a constant source of anxiety for me, ebbing and flowing throughout the years. Recently, it came crashing down in an irrational and overwhelming fear, fueling an already out-of-control anxiety.

While my son experienced a relatively normal childhood, my daughter's story is a bit different and full of incredible strength and courage. She had to overcome more than her fair share of obstacles to break free from her childhood and young adulthood. At age two, her mother and I were divorced. Our marriage had been unhappy for me. I did not feel honest about my feelings and felt from the beginning that I had been trapped in the marriage. It was a "shotgun" wedding, if you will, one that came about from pregnancy.

After the divorce, my ex-wife and I shared the responsibilities of care for our daughter, taking turns and passing each other in the exchange. I had given up the house in the divorce so that my daughter would have a home to live in. Her mother was a waitress working nights, and I worked for an insurance company during the day. We split shifts, as it were. My ex-wife would care for our daughter during the daytime, and I would come over at night to hang out, feed her, and put her to bed. I would stay there until her mother got off of work, then leave and go back to living on the streets in my 1970 VW Bus, and eventually various small, substandard apartments.

This arrangement, however, began to feel a lot like our marriage, the only difference being that we were lawfully divorced. I felt as though I needed to have some boundaries and set up limits as to when I would care for our daughter. A selfish decision, I know, and an incredibly difficult decision for me, and to this day, I sometimes regret it. Nevertheless, I set parameters: I would have my daughter every other weekend and two days during the week. This did not go over well with my ex-wife, but I felt it was necessary for me to have a chance at some sort of independent life. Ultimately, I knew that this would result in her mother having to find some form of childcare, and to be honest, I did not have a lot of faith in her ability to do so. This made the decision even harder because I worried about what kind of care my daughter would get.

It was difficult to have my daughter over at my apartment because it was small and not the nicest place to live. In fact, it was really quite nasty, with orange shag carpet, one single bed, and a shared bathroom for the entire floor. On my two days of custody during the week, I would still go to our home and wait for Lauren's mother to come home from work. After a while of this arrangement, I began to grow increasingly concerned about the care, or lack of care, that Lauren's mother was providing. Her mother would spend most of her mornings sleeping in, leaving Lauren on her own. I found out that some of my ex-wife's male friends were babysitting Lauren during the evenings. I would occasionally see a pair of men's shoes at the front entryway to the house when I came to pick my daughter up.

I know that I put a strain on my ex-wife's life, forcing her to find care for our daughter so she could work. I also knew that my ex-wife was entitled to live her life however she chose. I just spent a lot of time worrying about our daughter. I decided to look for a good daycare for my daughter so she could have some consistency of care during the day. After a few weeks, I found one. The only problem was that I couldn't afford it. I was struggling with money at the time, paying child support, rent, and the car payment for our car, which I had given to my ex-wife. During the early times of our divorce, I was driving and living in my 1970 VW Bus, with no heat or defrost system to speak of, or for that matter, adequate safety belts.

I had been talking with my mother about this entire situation and my worries for many weeks, and she wanted to help in some way. So, my dear mother came to the rescue and agreed to pay for daycare. I would now pick Lauren up every morning and take her to daycare at The Children's Garden. I would then pick her up after work and take her to her home. Things seemed to be okay for a while.

Her mother went through several relationships during this time and eventually met a man whom she decided to marry. Unfortunately, they would be moving to Omaha for his work. So, at the age of about seven or eight, my daughter was taken two hours away to another city to live with her mother and new stepfather. This, of course, made it difficult for me to see her on a regular basis. I would travel up on some weekends, and we would go to the zoo or some local playland or farmers' market. One time we went to a cat show. Sometimes I would take Lauren home to Des Moines to stay with me on the weekend, and I eventually bought a house. She would also stay with me during part of her summers. We would often travel to my mother's house in North Carolina to spend a week at the beach with grandma.

Any time I had to take her back home, it was heartbreaking and extremely difficult for both of us. She never made a big deal out of it, but I knew it had to be hard for her. I hated to leave her, and I always felt a dark void of aloneness and sadness afterward. It was a tragedy, really, a tragedy that I simply stuffed down into my emotional gullet.

Later, when my daughter was an adult, she expressed how difficult it was for her to see my son enjoying his dad full time and her feeling somewhat cheated, missing out on something she unfortunately did not get to experience.

After a couple of years, my ex-wife's marriage soured, and the stepfather became somewhat violent at times. They divorced, and my daughter was put through another traumatic experience. The mere fact that she lived with her mother for so many years was no picnic, as it became clear that my daughter had become the adult figure of the two, and her mom relied heavily on the poor kid for far more emotional support than any child should have to give a parent. Of course, I was going through a few relationships as well, and Lauren met all of my serious girlfriends at various ages in her life until I became engaged and married.

My daughter has grown up to be quite an amazing woman, and I am so proud of all the things that she has done, including moving to Seattle and freeing herself from the emotional chains of her mother. I still feel as if we both missed out on a lot, but we are close I think even though she lives so far away. I am terribly afraid she is a little too much like me in some respects. When we talk with each other it's a little scary how much our senses of humor are alike. It's a fine line between being a father and a friend. I think because we missed out on our time together when she was young, I lost a little fatherly cred if you will. Yet, I feel very close to her. She is definitely very sarcastic, and sees the world much like me. But she can laugh at it, and we both laugh at it when we talk on the phone. She is a thinker for sure, very intelligent and very beautiful. When Lauren was about six I took her to church thinking I should introduce her to religion. I'm not sure why, it just seemed like the thing a parent should do. As I was walking down the hallway to pick her up I heard a sweet little voice asking, "But what if there is no God?" It was both an extremely proud moment and a painfully scary one. At a very early age my daughter was questioning the existence of God. She worries me. A lot!

Today I had a break from the anxiety for a few hours. Life can be good, if only for a brief moment—or at least vacant from self-evaluation and awareness. On the way to taking my son to a church group, he played "Stairway to Heaven" by Led Zeppelin (of course!), and we turned it up loud, sang, and played drums in the car the whole way there. It was so wonderful to just be in the moment. I must remember that moment.

It is possible for me to be normal again, to drop the anxiety, and just enjoy the moment. I love my son so much it hurts. I see the infinite possibilities for my son. I have to be positive for him. It is the only reason I get out of bed some days.

I am slipping, slipping into a scary place where I can find no motivation. Everything is too overwhelming, so I do very little. I must learn to pretend again. When you wake up every morning with a feeling of nothingness and dread, just getting out of bed seems impossible. Making it through the day is difficult. I feel as if I know what's going to happen in our future. There are no surprises, nothing to look forward to, and no thrill.

I cannot play along anymore. I cannot pretend that everything is going to be alright. I cannot ignore what is going on around me. I feel like giving up. I am not good to be around.

I hide in our own house, away from my son, so he cannot see me in this condition.

I can't seem to shake it off. Is this version of me better for my family than an absent me? I sometimes think they would be better off without me around. Strength, I must find it. I must pretend and play along.

Right now, I am getting ready to work at a health food grocery store. I am full of anxiety. *I don't want to go. The anxiety is overwhelming. I must walk out the door. I must get in the car.* I turn on the car with the garage door closed, and I linger there for a minute, two, three. *I can't do this to my family.* Somehow, I manage to open the garage door and drive to work.

When I get there, I float above myself, watching, screaming. All I feel is intense fear. I am hollow, greeting people, functioning on some sub-human level. I pretend to be present. I am not.

I don't feel good.

Moving to Des Moines

"The 'S's' are silent"
-me

I was flying on a plane by myself at the age of twelve, crying. I was trying not to let anyone see me cry. Fortunately, I had a window seat, so I just leaned forward and looked out the window, sobbing quietly for most of the trip. That was how I left Langhorne, Pennsylvania, and ended up in Des Moines, Iowa. I really didn't want to leave; my life was pretty good there.

My dad had accepted the pastor position at the First Presbyterian Church of Des Moines, Iowa. My parents had moved at the end of my school year, but I stayed behind because my baseball team was going to the state all-star tournament a few weeks later than the moving date. I stayed with my teammate John and his family, who graciously put me up, fed me, and even took me to the shore with them for vacation.

We were a good team—a very good team. I was an all-star catcher who rarely, if ever, let a ball get by me. I also had a rocket for an arm, and no one could steal on me. I was third in the pitcher rotation with a sidearm delivery and a batting average of .461. Not bad, but I was the third-best hitter on the team. The two better than me batted .486, and my friend John batted .681. We were good! Really good!

We got written up in the *Philadelphia Enquirer* with four pictures and a lot of hype. Even though they misspelled my name twice, it was still pretty cool for a twelve-year-old. We finished the season 19-1 and thought we were bad ass. We went to the all-star tournament confident and expecting to win. John, our best pitcher, would be the starter, and I, of course, was the catcher.

We got blown out 12-1. It was over before we knew it. Every kid on the other team looked like they were eighteen years old. They lit John up from the beginning with six runs in the first inning. One kid hit a three-run homer that would have cleared a major league fence. It was brutal! We couldn't hit their pitcher, and they hit everything. I had the only RBI with a broken-bat single and ended up pitching the final two innings.

I don't remember much about my feelings after the game. I just knew that I would be going to my new home in Des Moines, Iowa, and that my life was going to change.

One of the worst things about my childhood was that I was a bed wetter. I wet the bed until I was twelve years old! It sucked! I didn't do it every night, but I definitely did it often. My parents used to wake me up in the middle of the night to try and help. They even took me to a doctor to see if there was something wrong with me. There wasn't, but needless to say, this condition made it almost impossible for me to ever spend the night at a friend's house.

So, staying with my teammate John's family was very stressful for me. If

I wet the bed, I would try to cover it up by throwing the sheets in the dryer in the middle of the night, or even going so far as to iron the wet sheets dry. It was a disaster, but I don't really remember ever discussing the issue with John's parents. Maybe they knew what was going on but didn't want to make me feel bad. Perhaps I have blocked it out or forgotten it; I really don't remember.

It finally went away, coincidentally, when I moved to Des Moines.

I remember flying into Des Moines and seeing the golden dome of the state capitol building. That's about it. My parents picked me up at the airport and we arrived at our new home, or should I say old manse. For those of you who don't know what a manse is, it is a home that is owned by the church but is the residence of the pastor and his family. It was a nice house made of brick, kind of a Tudor style with metal awnings in the front and a big tree. My parents had the master bedroom on the second floor, and I got the bedroom on the main floor. I'm not sure why or how this happened, but I kind of liked it for sneaking out at night. We lived on the east side of Des Moines, a blue collar lower middle-class part of town that I later learned was kind of looked down upon by those who lived in the western part of Des Moines. I, of course, didn't know the difference, since I wasn't from there. They now have an "east side night" at the state fair every year which is on one hand a novelty pride kind of a celebration for the east siders, but also a white trash kind of a night for anyone not from the east side.

I think I may have been a little depressed that first summer in Des Moines. I didn't know anyone and didn't do much. My mother got me this really weird gift that summer, which is kind of strange when I think about it. I don't even know what to call it, other than a kind of easy stitching kit for kids. I somehow managed to finish it with the needle and yarn that came in the kit. It said "Home Sweet Home." It came with a cheap, cheesy plastic brown frame, and my mother proudly put it up on the wall. Strange. Very strange indeed. I must have been a bit desperate.

My first year at May Goodrell Junior High School was rough. I remember having to walk a couple of miles in the morning. Mind you, I was thirteen years old. I don't even remember my parents being present during my junior high school days. By the way, who lets their thirteen-year-old kid walk two miles to school in the morning in today's world? I eventually began to hitchhike to school. I usually got picked up by nice, normal people who may have felt sorry for me, or were concerned for my safety. Sometimes it was even parents with kids from my school who picked me up. I don't know if my parents knew that I was doing this. Again, NO SUPERVISION!

It wasn't that big of a deal to me until one day these two young dudes picked me up extremely high from sniffing glue. They asked me if I wanted to try it, but I said no thanks. They were planning on robbing some store or something, but they dropped me off at school nevertheless. It was a little unnerving, to say the least. Yet, I continued to hitchhike to school.

School itself was filled with terror and fear. First, there were the ninth-grade boys, who would take off their belts and whip you with them if they caught you in the stairways. Then there was gym class, the dreaded gym class that was taught by none other than a man named Mr. Savage. Swear to God, that was his name. Let me tell you, gym class in the 1970s was not only hard, it was downright dangerous.

Let's start with the gym shorts. They were short; I mean really short, dangerously short. and you were required to wear them. We had to climb a 20-foot rope with a thin mat at the bottom in case we fell. I was never able to make it to the top, but almost every single time I attempted it, I received severe rope burns. The peg board was extremely difficult and looked like something from *American Ninja Warrior.* Not to mention sit-ups, push-ups, and pull-ups. Dodgeball was extremely dangerous for the uncoordinated, as ruthlessness and violence were almost encouraged.

By far, the worst thing about gym class was the required communal shower after class. This brought the full horrible nightmare crashing down on me. Being naked in front of twenty-seven other kids at the age of thirteen ranks as one of the cruelest tortures you can imagine for someone at such a tender age. For some kids, it was no problem at all. For me, it was sheer psychological horror. While I enjoyed a lot of the actual sports we played in gym class, the shower scene may have done irreparable damage to my psyche.

Then there were the ninth-grade girls. These girls were very aggressive, and they seemed to enjoy hunting their innocent, frightened seventh-grade prey. There was one girl in particular named Gigi, who was totally after me. Just her name terrified me. I had no idea about girls at this time and was frightened to death of them. Somehow, one night we hooked up at a friend's house and made out, and by that, I mean kissing and maybe some fondling. I must have been pretty bad at it, because I never heard from Gigi after that night. It's noteworthy to mention that my fear of women continued for most of my adult life. I was always painfully shy and never felt confident about approaching them or asking for dates.

Finally, there was this ninth-grade dude named Steve, who was rumored to be after me all fucking year long. People would always tell me, "Steve's after you, man, he's going to mess you up." Now, Steve was a big dude with long hair, and he seemed like a pretty mellow guy from a distance. After having spent the entire school year in fear, one day it happened in the front hallway of the school. Steve and I finally met by chance, and a crowd had somehow gathered around us, egging us on. Steve threw the first punch, and I remember ducking and just throwing wild punches without looking, until finally he kneed me in the face.

All I remember after that was being in the principal's office with Steve crying, and me not really knowing what happened. I always thought it was ironic that he was the one crying, yet I was the one who got the shit beat out of me. Our parents were called, and we were sent home for three days' suspension. I had a major black eye.

There were some other unpleasant moments, such as the time I fell headfirst into a huge industrial fan and received a concussion while running at the indoor track at the YMCA. I also had mononucleosis and an ingrown toenail that required surgery.

It got better after that, though, as I began to be considered one of the "cool kids." I was on the basketball team and was even elected "prom king" of the school in ninth grade. I was to accompany the school queen to the dance and be crowned alongside her. Unfortunately, I consumed way too much Boonesville Farms wine that night and never made it to the ceremony because I was too busy puking my guts out outside the school.

I did some crazy things during this time. I began to drink and do drugs. Sometimes my friends and I would steal drugs from our parents and take them. We didn't even know what we were taking half the time. One time a friend of mine gave me a pill at school, and I could not stay awake. The teacher put me in the hallway, and I sprawled out on the floor and fell asleep. My parents were called, and I told them I just didn't feel good.

My friend Gary and I would drink, smoke weed, and even drop acid. Mind you, this was in eighth and ninth grade. One time, we dropped some acid at Gary's house right before dinner, and it hit right at the dinner table. We were laughing, giggling, and losing it right there in front of his mom. Later that night, we stole his mom's Chevy Nova, carefully pushing it out of the garage into the street, and then starting it up. We drove around town all night long, tripping balls. It's a miracle we didn't kill someone or ourselves.

Gary and I also had this shoplifting record business. We stole hundreds of records from a local drug store and then sold them to the Foosball Parlor up the street or kept them ourselves. It was a carefully orchestrated crime, of which I am not proud. We would both find the records we wanted and move them up to the record section closest to the door. When we had finally gathered the records, one of us would walk out of the electric gate, making sure the coast was clear, while the other would grab the records, stash them underneath his coat, and walk quickly out the door.

Once out the door, we ran like hell to the designated hiding spot behind a garage. We would then sell some of the records to the local Foosball Parlor for cash. As I said before, I am not proud of this thievery, as I have always tried to limit myself to committing as few of the seven deadly sins as possible. I definitely failed the stealing sin.

I have stolen a few things in my younger years, including cigarettes, girly magazines, an electric guitar, and a golf glove. I was actually caught stealing the golf glove, as it was my first attempt at shoplifting. I was at the Richman Gordman store in my neighborhood and spent way too long getting up the nerve to actually shoplift, so I was easily identified. I actually made it out of the store and down the street when a car pulled up behind me and nabbed me.

I was taken to a room above the department store, where the police were called as well as my parents. I was banned from ever shopping at Richman Gordman, my criminal record would go away when I reached the age of sixteen, and my parents were extremely distraught. I remember my dad saying, "Why didn't you just ask us to buy the damn thing for you?" I don't know why I didn't "just ask." I should have, but I didn't.

Bumper sliding was a risky, dangerous, and thrilling activity that we often did in the winter. After a good snowfall, we would meet up at night and hide near a stop sign or traffic signal. As a car stopped, we would sneak behind it and grab onto the bumper. The snow on the street was just right for sliding. The risk came from not knowing where the car was going or how skilled the driver was. You had to let go of the bumper at the right moment, or you could get seriously hurt.

I'm not sure who came up with the idea, and it's not like we knew how to do it. We just tried it because it seemed fun. One time, my glove got stuck in the bumper, and I couldn't get it free, so I had to pull my hand out of the glove. Later, we happened upon the same car in the Walgreens parking lot, with my glove still stuck in the bumper. What luck!

Another rather dangerous thing I did by myself was jump trains. I would walk to the train yard near our house, find a slow-moving train, and jump on for a ride. Jumping off the train was probably the most dangerous part because you never knew how fast it was going or what the terrain would be like. Walking back on the tracks was therapeutic—balancing on the rails as long as I could, trying to jump from one rail to the other without falling. And just walking in rhythm with the tracks felt calming.

It seems like these years, from ages 13 to 18, were filled with danger, temptation, and forks in the road. Drugs and alcohol slowly but surely began to creep into my life. I remember telling myself I would never do drugs or smoke cigarettes, and I did fight them off for a while. It was in eighth grade that I finally succumbed. I can't even remember the first time I smoked weed. I think it was while camping in my neighbor's backyard, but I can't be sure.

I remember my friend Gary and I getting beer. I hated the taste at first, probably because we were drinking Pabst Blue Ribbon, Falstaff, and Old Milwaukee. I remember the numb sensation in my lips. We used to hang out at Grandview Golf Course at night, drinking on the 6th or 7th tee—I don't remember which. Pretty soon after that, we were smoking weed regularly.

Good weed, too! We had choices: Thai Stick, Panama Red, Columbian Gold, Jamaican, and the worst, Mexican. Hash and hash oil with white opium stripes. We dropped acid a few times—all the while managing to stay out of trouble.

Until one night, a group of friends and I scored an ounce of Columbian Gold and split it four ways, $25 a piece. We drove out to the country on some dirt road and were toking when two state patrol cars pulled up behind us. We were fucked! Somehow, by the grace of God, they let us go. They made us dump all of our weed on the ground and told us to just go home and don't come back. I don't think that would happen today.

There was another time when I got busted. My friend Gary and I decided to buy a pound of weed to sell. He got caught by his mom and uncle, and he told them I was in on it too. They came to our house, and I confessed. I remember feeling really bad about it and dumping the weed down the toilet in front of my parents, vowing to give it up. I mean, I really felt bad. Today, I probably would have been sent to therapy, drug rehab, or worse. But my parents trusted me and let me figure things out myself. That was one thing they always did—they trusted me. They may not have been there all the time, but they definitely loved and trusted me.

And I let them down badly this time. Did I give up smoking weed? NO, I did not. But something changed for me that day. Something was different.

I had a couple of different jobs during my middle school and early high school years. My first job was as a paperboy. I delivered the afternoon paper and the Sunday paper. The Sunday paper was the worst, it was super heavy, and I had to get up at 4:00 a.m. Sometimes it was pouring rain or freezing cold, and my dear mother would get up to drive me around.

I had a red wagon to help with the deliveries. Early Sunday morning, I would fold and rubber-band the papers, load them into the wagon, and off I went. The route ended at the top of an extremely steep, long hill, so I would ride the red wagon down at times, barely maintaining control. It was reckless but an adrenaline rush. Getting up early on Sundays eventually got old, so I quit. Being out there in the early hours was also very scary—I kept my eyes open and moved as fast as I could.

There is a famous true story of a paperboy named Johnny Gosch, who was kidnapped while delivering his morning paper route in 1982 in West Des Moines. This happened long after my paper route days, but the event signaled the end of young kids delivering papers. The kidnapping also led to pictures on milk cartons and a heightened awareness of the dangers of pedophiles and child abductions. Johny's mother kept searching for many years. Some viewed her as overly obsessed, but her advocacy led to a bill allowing authorities to investigate a missing child immediately, rather than waiting 72 hours.

Although Johnny was never found, his mother claimed he visited her 15 years after the kidnapping. The story goes that Johnny knocked on her door, accompanied by a stranger. He spoke with his mother for an hour but said he was still in serious danger. Then he left and was never heard from again.

Speaking of walking home in the dark and being scared to death, I had a friend who worked at the old Galaxy Theater in downtown Des Moines. The Galaxy Theater was built in 1913 and was the first building to have a neon sign in Des Moines. It was a beautiful ornate theater that had originally been used for vaudeville acts. It went through many changeovers, and was close to demolition in 1977 when a friend and I snuck in the back door to the balcony for free. The movie we saw that night was the original *Texas Chainsaw Massacre*. It was my first experience with the genre of Horror. It frightened me to death.

After it was over, for some reason I had to walk home from downtown to the east side by myself. It was an intensely terrifying walk...or run, home in the dark. I imagined chainsaw murderers hiding around every corner and alleyway. I would run as fast as I could, then stop to catch my breath, constantly looking behind me and around me, only to be gripped by terror again. I would run full speed until I was out of breath, then repeat the pattern. This went on for miles, through downtown alleys, side streets, and unfamiliar neighborhoods.

I don't think my parents knew where I was for half of my childhood, especially during my teen years.

When I was 14 I got a job as a busboy at the Holiday Inn, Top of the Tour restaurant in downtown Des Moines. The center of the restaurant turned very slowly, giving diners a panoramic view of the skyline of the "beautiful" city of Des Moines while they ate. I failed miserably at this job, dropping an entire tray of dirty dishes and spilling water on guests as I tried to pour it.

It was a somewhat classy restaurant, so I had to carry the dirty dishes on a tray like a waiter would carry food, held at the side and elevated by my head. One time, I had a full tray of dirty dishes and completely dropped the entire thing. I'm not sure if I quit or was fired, but the job didn't last long.

That same year, there was a horrible murder at the hotel's front desk. In August 1974, two employees were killed during an apparent robbery in which only $269 was stolen. The crime remains unsolved to this day.

Although the crime happened at 2:00 am long after the restaurant closed, it still kind of freaks me out a little. I used to walk by that front desk on my way to and from work at night.

I had a busboy job at a local restaurant called the Steak and Show, located across the street from the famous Anderson & Erickson Dairy company. The restaurant had a strange theme. They played Don Ho videos—you know, the famous Hawaiian singer—on TV screens as entertainment while guests dined on hamburgers and steaks.

I swear the owners were Greek and spoke with thick accents. If you've ever seen the *Saturday Night Live* skit with Jim Belushi and Dan Aykroyd running the burger joint, you'd notice the uncanny similarity to the Steak and Show. They only served Coke products, so when a customer asked for a Pepsi, they would respond, "No Pepsi, just Coke!"

I used to ride my bike home from this job late at night down a busy road. One night, I noticed a car bumper dangerously close to my back tire. Before I could even turn around, I was knocked off my bike by someone's fist hitting me in the jaw. I heard them laughing as they sped off. That was the last time I went to work at that job. I guess I was lucky not to have been run over.

Then there was my sacking job at the Hinky Dinky, a grocery store that has long since disappeared. It was a decent gig and kept me and my friends supplied with Marlboro Reds. I used to steal cartons of cigarettes regularly. Yes, I had been smoking since the age of 16—not a lot, but consistently. Back then, it was just the cool thing to do.

Next, I worked at Adventureland, the large amusement park just outside of Altoona, Iowa. I was at Soda and Sounds, a strange little hamburger joint where a band would rise up out of the floor every hour to perform pop songs of the '70s, Captain and Tennille, Carly Simon, and others I can't quite remember. It was there that I developed a desire to play guitar, and start a band.

I worked most of the summer, sometimes running arcade games but mostly cooking French fries at Soda and Sounds. My goal was to buy my first electric guitar and amp—and I did it. I got an Electra red sunburst with a whammy bar and a cheap little amp. My parents helped a bit, but I earned most of it myself.

I took a few lessons at the local Lee Town Music Shoppe, but I mostly taught myself. I'd put on my favorite records and spend hours learning the songs I loved, Led Zeppelin, Black Sabbath, Tommy Bolin, David Bowie, and others. After school and all summer long, that was all I did. I got pretty good.

High school was worse than middle school. I had to ride the stupid bus as a freshman for the first few weeks, and it was horrible. Riding the bus in high school is right up there with some of the worst things you could experience—slightly below divorce and moving.

I attended East High School, located right on Interstate 235 off 14th Street. I was pretty miserable at first, but then I ran into Lumpy in biology class. That wasn't his real name, of course, but everyone called him that because he had been chubby as a kid. I made him laugh in class one day by pretending to make out with a girl in the back of the room—you know, putting your arms around yourself and turning your back so it looks like you're kissing. He was super high, so he laughed, and we became good friends.

I found out he played the drums, and I was a guitarist. He also drove a VW Bug and offered to pick me up in the mornings, which got me off the stupid bus. We began jamming in my garage, starting with "Iron Man" by Black Sabbath. Eventually, we found a singer and rehearsed in the sanctuary of my dad's church, it had a PA system and amazing acoustics.

The band never really amounted to much. I went off to college, and the others got full-time jobs.

Lumpy and I rode to East High School every morning in his VW Bug. This was no ordinary Bug—it was tricked out and supercharged. Lumpy worked on it constantly to make it faster and look cooler. He drove like a bat out of hell, and some rides were harrowing, to say the least. Every morning, we would merge onto the freeway at about 80 MPH. Sometimes I would be so scared that I would scream at him to slow down—or even let me out. Should have died many times during those years.

Underneath the passenger seat was a purple triple-bubble bong that we would hit every morning on the way to school. We'd be totally wasted and then go straight to first-period gym, running our asses off at basketball most days.

There is very little I remember about high school besides smoking marijuana, partying, and girls. Partying was constant. We smoked before school, at lunch, and after school. I was stoned all the time. On weekends, we would go to parties, or sometimes just drive around and party in Lumpy's Bug.

We occasionally got in trouble. Often, we would find someone to buy us beer and head to Grand View Park, where we'd drink, smoke, and jam out to tunes on Lumpy's kick-ass stereo. One night, some girls met us in the park, and we were having a good time when the cops showed up. They found our beer, but thankfully not our weed. We were all arrested for underage possession of alcohol. We were fingerprinted, had mug shots taken, and put in a large holding cell to await our parents bailing us out.

While in the cell, I found a small bag of weed tucked between the wall and the door frame. My father was pissed when he got a call from the police. I think he wanted to leave me there all night, but instead, he let me stew for a couple of hours. I imagine my mom ordered him to go get me out.

Things didn't change much after that. We still partied and carried on. It wasn't good, but it was fun at the time. My criminal record could be expunged if I stayed out of trouble for the next five years, and I did. To my knowledge, my record is clean.

We used to do some crazy stuff; "we" meaning Lumpy, myself, another friend Chuck, and a few others whose names I can no longer remember. There was this giant spillway out at Big Creek, north of the city. We had heard stories about rope swings that dropped into the water and people sliding down the spillway itself. Naturally, we went out there many times. It was an unforgettable rush.

The rope swings were a blast, but the spillway was the real thrill ride. It was a steep, 100-yard diagonal wall of concrete, slick with slime and just a trickle of water. At the bottom was a small pond, a collection area for excess water when the man-made lake on the other side overflowed.

We would sit on our butts and slide down at breathtaking speeds. There was very little control, you had to rely on your hands to keep yourself facing forward. Facing forward was crucial at the bottom, because you had to lift your legs slightly as you hit the pond to hydroplane safely. Miss it, and you could get seriously hurt.

Eventually, someone did. I wasn't there, but I heard they hit the bottom at the wrong angle, struck their head, and drowned. That tragic accident ended our spillway adventures. Afterward, the authorities fenced the area completely, making it impossible to reach.

Still, I can't forget that adrenaline, the rush of sliding down the slick, shining concrete, the screams of excitement, and the dangerous thrill that made us feel alive. It was reckless, terrifying, and unforgettable…. all at the same time.

We used to go to Gray's Lake to swim. It was a large lake on the south side of town, long before they built the nice walkway around it or started renting boats. Back then, there weren't any designated swimming areas, just open water and a lot of freedom.

One time, a group of us decided to swim straight across the lake, widthwise. It was stupid and risky, but we didn't care. I remember getting tired halfway across and feeling cramps start to set in. Our breathing was heavy, and we had to stop occasionally to tread water or float, just to conserve energy.

Somehow, against all odds, we all made it to the other side. The exhaustion was real, but so was the sense of accomplishment. Looking back, it was reckless, but thrilling, a memory of testing ourselves in a way that only seemed possible back then.

Then we swam back. Later that year a high school friend of ours named David tried to do the very same thing and didn't make it. I didn't know him that well, but we partied together a few times. He was a nice guy. Never could swim in that lake again.

Sometimes we would explore rock quarries outside of town. We discovered this awesome one with small cliffs to jump off and super clean and clear water. We would bring tubes and beer and hang out all day. No one would bother us. It was like having your own private lake. We would even take our girlfriends (if we had one) out there. Eventually private property signs began to appear, and guards were put on patrol. We got kicked out several times and threatened with police action, so we stopped going to our own private lake.

I never actually had a real girlfriend in high school until my senior year, when I met a girl from another school at a party. Sure, I had gone out with a girl or two before, but I was scared shitless of girls. I didn't have sex until I was 18, which felt late at the time; most of my friends were getting laid much earlier. I have to admit, I was just plain scared. I was never very outgoing around girls; they usually had to come to me, because I certainly didn't go to them. I didn't have the nerve to make the first move or try to "pick one up," as it was called back then. Lack of confidence was always an issue.

Anyway, one night, Lumpy and I heard about a party at the Adventureland Hotel, which had an indoor pool and a bar. Pretty sure we weren't invited, we didn't know anyone there. After a while, we found ourselves sitting at a table with a group of good-looking girls from Southeast Polk High School, a kind of country school outside Des Moines in Altoona, Iowa. We started talking, comparing notes about high school life, and I suggested showing them some of the cool places to go in Des Moines, like sledding down the 10th-hole fairway at Grandview Golf Course.

I got every girl to write down her name and phone number on a piece of paper. Then came the hard part: figuring out which one to call first. To be honest, I think the girl third from the left was the nicest and most attractive, but I wasn't sure the numbers were in order. An ambiguous and random fork in the road. A major fork in the road. Tempting fate like a Greek tragedy.

As it turns out, the name I chose to call from the list was Jani's. We ended up dating for seven years and came damn near to getting married. We were together from the time I was 17 until I was 24. She was the only girl I really knew or experienced in my young adult life.

When I think about how different my life would have been if I'd married Jani at the ripe age of 25, I shudder, both in a bad way and a good way. I would never have experienced the things that came after our breakup, but I would have lived a very "normal" life. Maybe. You see, these forks in the road, the ambiguity; they keep appearing throughout my life. You rarely notice them at the time. In fact, you often don't recognize their life-changing potential until much later, like when you're writing a book or journaling.

It's kind of like horrible things that are unbearable in the moment but, in hindsight, become amusing or endearing. Like raising a child—it's mostly hell at the time—but later you remember the difficult moments fondly, as part of the journey.

Jani and I did a lot together. We went to her prom. We traveled to concerts. We went to college together and practically lived together at the University of Iowa. We lost our virginity together. We got to know each other's families well. We spent Christmases together. We vacationed together. It seemed like we were meant to marry.

But nope. I took the other road.

Small Town

"I used to love the idea of small towns. Now they scare me to death."

-me

Donnellson, Iowa, is located in the southeast corner of the state. It's a small town that, at the time, had a population of about 800. There was a school, a local doctor, one gas station, a bar, a small privately-owned grocery store, and a Dairy Freeze (a soft-serve ice cream shop). My Aunt Alta, Aunt Edna, and Uncle Harbin all lived there. All of my aunts (three in total) as well as my mother were born and raised in Donnellson.

It was, and probably still is, a small town with simple living at its finest. To me, it was pure goodness: good food, card games, Fourth of July fireworks, fishing, parades, and wholesomeness. I loved going there as a child.

Once, I took a train with my mother and sisters all the way from Miami, Florida, to Fort Madison, Iowa. I couldn't have been more than eight or nine years old. It was an amazing trip! We ate in the restaurant car, had our own cabin with fold-out bunks, a little bathroom, and a sink. There was one car called the observation car, where you could go up to a second level and watch the countryside go by. It was fascinating to me.

We stayed in Donnellson for a few weeks during that summer trip. My grandmother was still alive then, and she had a huge garden and a big old cherry tree that I would climb to pick cherries, but mostly to eat them. Her house was extremely large, with a lovely porch swing, built-in cabinets, and red oak hardwood floors.

My Uncle Harbin and Aunt Edna lived across the street in a house Harbin had built himself. He was an incredible inventor and all-around fixer, a true tinkerer. He had created an electric rod that brought up nightcrawlers for fishing. He had all sorts of fascinating things, including liquid mercury and an old TV with a blue magnifying glass over the screen. He helped me make boats and planes from scraps of wood, took me bass fishing at a friend's farm pond, and even let me drive his car on a dirt road when I was twelve.

Sometimes we would go to Frankie's Pond. Frankie was my Aunt Alta's longtime boyfriend. He was a farmer who always wore overalls. My aunt never married him, fearing she would have to take care of him; he had diabetes and didn't take care of himself. Frankie would hook up his tractor to a trailer and take us to his pond, which was stocked with bass. It was quite the occasion.

On one of these fishing trips, my Uncle Harbin was removing a hook from a largemouth bass when the fish jumped suddenly, driving the hook deep into his finger. He couldn't remove it because it had hooked underneath the bone. We went home, where he carefully cut and manipulated the hook out using a razor blade and pliers. I watched him do it. He didn't even consider going uptown to see the doctor. I was fascinated by the grotesque, bloody "surgery."

Another time, my uncle helped put out a grease fire on a neighbor's stove. He burned his finger badly, and the blister was enormous, literally half the size of his finger. Again, he never went to the doctor. I adored my Uncle Harbin.

Harbin was married to my Aunt Edna, whose sole purpose in life seemed to be centered around food and cooking. The meals that she prepared were legendary sometimes taking the full day to make. As a kid I was amazed at all the foods to choose from at meal time. Aunt Edna was the oldest of all the sisters on my mother's side. She seemed very happy and somewhat simple-minded. She and Harbin had no children so they loved when our family would visit.

My Aunt Alta, on the other hand, was a perfect storm of obsessive-compulsive tendencies, perfectionism, anxiety, and tragedy, the core traits behind many of the problems associated with our family genes. She was a high school principal who used the paddle on many occasions to enforce discipline at her Fort Madison School.

Aunt Alta was a miser and amassed a vast fortune over her lifetime, saving and investing so carefully that she left every living relative a generous inheritance, as well as a substantial donation to her church when she passed. Her personality was shaped, in part, by a tragic early love who left her for New York City. This heartbreak seemed to jade her for the rest of her life.

She spent her final years in the Donnellson nursing home, suffering from severe anxiety and Alzheimer's disease. She would mutter to herself, "that's age, that's age," in a mournful way that was almost unbearable to witness. Aunt Alta was a constant worrier from the first time I met her; a trait I recognize in myself, my mother and sisters all too well.

There were fleeting moments when she was funny, but they were brief. She was very hard of hearing, and her hearing aids rarely worked properly. They often whistled at ear-piercing frequencies, leaving her perpetually misunderstanding what was said or asked of her. Sometimes this was unintentionally amusing, as she would respond completely off-topic, much to the hilarity of others. Poor Aunt Alta!

She was constantly annoyed with her older sister, Aunt Edna, who was constantly concerned and occupied with what to serve for breakfast, lunch, and dinner. Besides being a wonderful cook, Aunt Edna was a dedicated gardener. She canned food religiously and had a fruit cellar full of goodies like dilly tomatoes, gooseberry jam, beets, and bread-and-butter pickles. She kept very busy, seemed quite content with her small-town life, and was genuinely happy.

The later years, however, were harsh. Uncle Harbin died suddenly of a heart attack, but mercifully. Aunt Edna, despite her zest for life, eventually ended up in the same Donnellson nursing home as her sister Alta after developing diabetes, breaking her hip, and losing her home and savings, relying on Medicaid to cover medical expenses. I always thought it terribly ironic that Aunt Edna, who lived with joy and energy, ended up in a nursing home with terrible food, while Aunt Alta, who prized independence, became a complete basket case due to Alzheimer's.

Was this karma? Was this some sort of natural reckoning or cosmic justice? Did the bill come due for the life my aunts had lived.? Was it that simple? Was I the only one to see this bitter irony as a lesson, a warning? Does everyone's life have this sort of karmic justice at the end? Ambiguity!

My dad's side of the family has remained relatively unknow to us. As I said before, my father believed that his mother suffered from depression. I never met her. On a lighter note, my father's father was at one time believed to be "the second oldest living twins in America," Floyd and Lloyd Sissel. I believe my grandfather was Floyd. He and his twin received letters from the President of the United States on their birthdays. I saw him a handful of times, and he would always give me five shiny brand-new pennies.

He lived in Whitefish, Montana, until the ripe old age of 99, leading a clean life, while his twin smoked cigars and drank a little. He on the other hand, lived to 102 Go figure. Perhaps there's a lesson in there.

Honesty, Control and Fatherly Advice

"Honesty is more than not lying. It is truth telling, truth speaking, truth living and truth loving."

-James E. Faust

I've always prided myself on being honest, with both myself and others. (With the exception of my thievery in my youth.) It has always been important for me to live my life with honesty. There have been many instances where telling the truth was extremely hard, moments that hurt others and cost me people I loved.

I think honesty is rare. It is often much easier to live a lie than to live the truth. Sometimes, the line between honesty and lies feels very grey. As you get older, that line can melt together so completely that you lose sight of the truth. It's not something you do on purpose—it just happens, as you try to convince yourself that everything is fine when it really isn't.

Life can feel a bit like smoke and mirrors, a kind of con game. We con ourselves into believing that we are being honest with ourselves when we are truly not. We like to assume that other people are being honest with us but we can never be sure. I'm pretty good at telling the difference between people that are honest and those who are not. They stick out very clearly to me. Loud people are generally not honest. I suspect that wealthy people, and those who seek power and influence, often sacrifice honesty. It seems to be a casualty of both wealth and power, replaced instead by greed, ambition and delusion.

Honesty can be sacrificed sometimes to make our life stories seem more interesting and exciting. In my case, there is a self-conscience task master that demands that I be honest and truthful. There are no exceptions, it is unforgiving and extremely judgmental, both of myself and of others. This honesty master is just another way for me to try and control my world. Control is what I seek, what I must have to feel safe. Of course, there is no such thing as control, the world is always changing, your world is always changing. It is perceived control that I'm after and what most people operate under. Not me, I've lost the feeling of perceived control, my world is out of control.

It is much easier to fool yourself into thinking you have control when you are single. It is much easier to manage truth and honesty when you are the only person you have to account for. Misery is much easier when you're alone and there are no witnesses. For those of us who crave control, marriage and children are the ultimate loss of it. But in place of control comes love, caring, and responsibility.

My son said to me tonight, "I suck at everything." It was a moment of sheer agony and sadness for me. Even though I could relate…. because that is exactly how I feel right now, hearing him say it broke my heart.

Please, God, don't let him be like me.

I tried to help, though I'm not sure I did. I told him he does not suck at everything. I told him he is good at many things, and that tennis, a sport he trains for and one we have invested in, does not define him. Neither do his stupid video games.

He gets very frustrated with his video games. So, do I. Sometimes he yells and screams. He slams his hands down on the desk and stomps around his room, causing our dog to cower in fear and filling me with anxiety.

I cannot relate to video games. I have no interest in them and no ability with them. Sometimes I want to walk into his room with a sledgehammer and smash all of his stupid gaming devices. His frustration reminds me of my own struggles with building models as a kid.

I told my son that someday he will find something he wants to work very hard at, and that he will be very good at it. I told him that if he decides to do something and truly commits to it, he can do anything he wants to do. I told him, "I believe in you," which I do.

I could have told him it is okay to be mediocre at many things and still have many different experiences. I could have told him to enjoy what life gives him and go after the things that make him happy.

But I didn't.

I could have told him to find something to devote himself to and become the very best he can at it. To not give up, and that someday he might find success through persistence.

I could have told him to pay attention to the forks in the road that life presents, to analyze his choices, weigh the possible outcomes, and choose the best path he can.

I could have told him that life is an adventure, and that he should try to have the best adventure possible.

I could have told him the importance of knowing where the clitoris can be found on a woman.

I could have told him to avoid becoming like his father at all costs.

Parenting sucks!

I think you know by now that I find life deeply ambiguous. There are no signposts that say, "This is the right way to go," or "This is the right thing to do."

Why can't there be signs?

Perhaps because any path can become the right one, thereby making all paths, in some sense, right. They are neither right nor wrong, neither bad nor good. They are simply the paths we take. This is the ultimate ambiguity, and ultimately, the ultimate burden of choice.

I'm not sure I can accept the idea that "life is what you make of it." I'm not sure it works that way for everyone, especially for the disadvantaged. I understand that the amount of effort you put into something often determines what you get out of it. But circumstances, options, choices, and the people you meet are, for the most part, random and ambiguous.

Some people seem able to roll with ambiguity and randomness. In fact, they may actually enjoy it. They find it exciting, challenging, maybe even freeing. It doesn't bother them in the least, perhaps because they don't look back on it very much.

How did I get so lucky?

Right now, I am faced with the task of finding a job.

Talk about ambiguity.

I currently work as a substitute postal delivery person—an RCA, Rural Carrier Associate. I hate it. I am not good at it, and I am about ready to quit or get fired, whichever comes first.

I have applied for several jobs, but I am struggling to find a niche at the ripe old age of fifty-eight. I have been a sixth-grade teacher for most of my adult life, and I know very little about other professions. I also don't really know what I'm qualified to do.

Looking for a job is right up there with divorce and moving on the list of "the worst things in life you could ever possibly do."

I am not the most confident person in the world these days. When you're depressed and anxiety-ridden, you don't exactly exude confidence.

Today is a very bad day.

Last night, my wife and I had an argument about money, and I woke up this morning feeling deeply depressed and overwhelmed by life. I had no motivation to do anything, so I went back to bed and stewed in my anxiety.

I feel like I am crawling out of my own skin—paralyzed by fear, overwhelmed by the infinite number of things that need to be done, and crushed by everything that feels wrong with our lives.

I think about what a bad parent I am. What a bad husband I am. The fact that I don't have a job. The fact that I have very few prospects. The debt we have accrued on our credit cards. Our inability to budget. All of it piles up until I can hardly breathe.

Taking my son to school today, I watched all the people in their cars, each one with a destination, a job, a place to go. They have purpose. They know what their day will look like.

I, on the other hand, have nothing.

I go home to nothing, nothing but a big reminder of the endless, meaningless tasks that need to be done. And then I feel so overwhelmed that I do nothing.

So, I write.

What else can I do?

I am seriously depressed.

I am having trouble getting out of bed. I am having trouble finding anything worthwhile. I have no zest for life. Nothing for life. I just go through the routine, trying to stay busy and trying not to worry too much about the future.

I applied for some jobs. One of them was a supply technician position in sterile supply at a hospital. They called me today and asked me to come in for an interview and to check out the job. After watching a few YouTube videos about the position, I don't think I'm interested.

It looks kind of scary.... being around surgical supplies, some of which have been used, cleaning and sterilizing them, and putting surgical kits together. I want to call the guy and cancel the interview. There is no way I can do that job, especially given the germaphobe I have become because of my autoimmune disease.

I was diagnosed with rheumatoid arthritis in my late fifties. It began as severe pain in both of my feet, so bad that it was extremely painful to walk. At first, I was diagnosed with plantar fasciitis. I received shots in my feet and even had one foot put in a cast, but nothing helped.

Then one morning, I woke up and my left pointer finger was swollen to three times its normal size. After that, my elbow swelled to the point that I could not move it. Eventually, my wrist became so painful that I could not move it either.

During this time, I was going to podiatrists, orthopedists, and physical therapists on a regular basis. I received several steroid shots in multiple places, but still nothing changed. After researching my symptoms online, I became fairly convinced of what the diagnosis was.

As a last-ditch effort, I went to my family doctor. He happened to be out the day of my appointment, so instead I saw an Eastern European doctor that I had never met before. He had tattoos all over his arms and even his neck. I told him, "There is something seriously wrong with me."

He actually listened.

Again, I was saved by a doctor. In the right place at the right time. Ambiguous and random for sure. Thank goodness for some random ambiguity.

He ordered a full workup of labs, especially tests for rheumatoid factors, and my diagnosis was pretty much confirmed. I was sent to a specialist, and my treatment began.

First, I was given a low dose of a chemotherapy-type drug, which I injected myself. It did not work and made me very sick. Then I was put on Enbrel, a drug that can cost tens of thousands of dollars a month. It is an injection I give myself every week.

Fortunately, our insurance covered the drug, and I began to improve to the point of feeling pretty much normal. I could play tennis again.

Had insurance not covered this medication, I might have ended up with severe joint damage, gnarled fingers and toes, and possibly a life spent in a wheelchair. That is the fate of many people who do not have insurance or cannot afford the drug. Fortunately, I was diagnosed early and did not suffer long-term damage to my joints.

When I tell people I have rheumatoid arthritis, they often say, "Oh, I have that too." But they are usually talking about regular arthritis and stiff joints. I'm sure that is painful, but it is not the same as rheumatoid arthritis.

With rheumatoid arthritis, my body's immune system attacks my joints. Left untreated, it can cause severe joint damage and deformities, along with problems involving the heart, lungs, and nervous system.

So, the drug I take suppresses my immune system. In effect, it turns it down. That makes it easier for me to get sick, and infections can become serious.

Being around biohazardous materials does not seem like a safe move for me.

I think I will cancel the interview. But I feel bad for wasting the man's time. And that makes me feel even more depressed, more hopeless, and less confident in everything.

Like Father Like Son

"We never know the love of a parent till we become parents ourselves."
-Henry Ward Beecher

Because my dad was bi-polar there were times when he would sit in his dark study and do nothing but smoke. I don't know what else he did in there. I didn't really understand the scope of his depression, or even depression itself. I thought he was just down, that was all. I guess I was too busy with my own teenage life, too self-absorbed. I also was completely ignorant of mental illnesses at the time.

One time, I tried to pull him out of feeling down (depression) by placing exploding caps in the tips of his cigarettes. When he lit them, they exploded and blew off the end of his cigarette. I did this for about a week. He did not find it nearly as funny as I did.

I was fifteen or sixteen at the time, and I was just trying to cheer him up.

No one really knew how to treat depression in the seventies, or maybe my dad did not seek help. Either way, my dad suffered greatly from his. Then he would go through manic stages, when he would stay up all night, ride his bike down to the 7-Eleven, and hang out with the night-shift employees.

The 7-Eleven was not exactly a safe place to be between two and five in the morning.

One time, he came home with his face all bloodied up. He had seen a man on a motorcycle who seemed to be having trouble starting it and asked if he needed help. The man walked over and hit my dad without saying a word.

When my dad was manic, he smoked and drank a lot, though there were very few times I actually saw him drunk. I don't know how he physically managed to smoke as many cigarettes as he did in a day, but at one point he was up to three packs a day.

He mostly drank bourbon and martinis. When I was very young, I asked if I could try a sip of his martini. Instead, he offered me the lemon peel twist soaked in gin, mistakenly thinking I wouldn't like it.

I loved it.

So, after he finished his martinis, I usually got the lemon peels.

What lesson was taught there? And what lesson was learned?

When I was 16, my parents decided to visit some old friends of theirs in Vermont. We drove from Des Moines to my sister's house in Doylestown, Pennsylvania, and stayed with her for a few days before continuing on to Vermont.

My dad planned the route and decided that driving through New York City would somehow be the fastest way to reach our destination. My dad was not a patient man when it came to driving, nor did he have a particularly keen sense of direction. He wanted to make as few stops as possible and make the best time possible, often at the expense of actually making the best time possible.

We had taken a few trips before from Des Moines to Rehoboth Beach, Delaware, with me crammed into the hatch of our Datsun and a luggage rack strapped to the top. Those trips were kick-ass long. Once, our luggage rack came apart while we were driving on Highway 80, spewing our clothing all over the roadside. We managed to gather most of our things and rig the luggage rack well enough to finish the trip.

On the trip from Philadelphia to Vermont, we were supposed to travel through some of the most densely populated areas of the country in order to save a few minutes.

It did not work out that way.

I didn't pay much attention to directions at the age of sixteen, but something told me that going through New York City was not going to be a shortcut.

My dad got lost.

We traveled endlessly through all four boroughs, and for some damn reason, we could not find our way out. We drove around for hours. My father became so angry and frustrated that he finally pulled over in front of a bar, parked the car, and left my mother and me sitting there while he went inside to have a drink.

We waited nervously for about an hour before he finally emerged. We begged him to ask for directions, and eventually convinced him. We happened upon a policeman, who gave us directions to the right highway.

Unfortunately, by then it had started pouring rain.

As we were crossing the George Washington Bridge, we got a flat tire. For some reason, I ended up changing it in the pouring rain, right there in the middle of the bridge. I don't know whether I volunteered because my dad was about to completely lose it, or whether he simply told me I had to get out there and do it.

I'm not even sure I knew how to change a flat tire at that time. But somehow, I figured it out, and we were on our way.

It made for quite a story when we finally arrived.

You know how experiences like that become amusing when told later, even though the actual experience was a living hell? That is a phenomenon I like to call "life."

Life is complicated. It is often horrible, sad, and challenging. Sometimes it is fun and exhilarating. But most of the time, it is just everyday living.

I graduated six months early from high school because I hated it.

I took night classes and earned the required credits so I could graduate without attending the second semester of my senior year. The counselor advised my parents not to let me do this, warning them that I would miss all the benefits of that final semester—Senior Prom and other things that did not matter to me.

My father told the counselor that I viewed high school as "a dark pit" and wanted to escape.

So, I left without so much as a goodbye.

I didn't get senior pictures. I didn't go to the senior prom. I simply left.

Then I got a job with a carpenter building houses. It was bitterly cold, hard work. Building houses in January and February in Iowa is difficult, to say the least. Let's just say I was not cut out for being a carpenter at that time.

I did not do very well and showed little promise, so I either quit or got fired.

I can't remember which.

At the beginning of the summer of 1978, my high school friend Gary and I decided we were going to hitchhike to California and back.

This was going to be a great adventure, or so we thought.

Our parents were not too thrilled with the idea, but they let us go, with some reservations. We packed our relatively small backpacks with sleeping bags, some clothes, a few snacks, two-gallon water jugs, and a small pocket atlas. I had about $250 in cash, and Gary brought about the same.

We had no real plan other than to make it to California and, hopefully, back.

My parents dropped us off just outside of Des Moines, where Interstate 80 West and Interstate 35 South converge. We stuck out our thumbs, and the adventure began.

We were first picked up by a nice man who was drinking whiskey. He offered us a sip, and we accepted.

Things were starting off great.

He drove us for quite a long way before we realized we were heading in the wrong direction. Unfortunately, we were going south toward Kansas City, not west.

An auspicious beginning, to say the least.

We got out, thanked him, crossed over to the other side of the highway, and started again, backtracking to where we had begun. We finally made it back and were picked up by a man headed to Colorado.

Now we were on our way.

He dropped us off in the middle of the Rocky Mountains at night. There were no towns in sight, and for a long time, no one stopped to pick us up. It was getting cold, and we were starting to worry.

Finally, a guy in a Ford Mustang pulled over. He said he was going to Salt Lake City.

We said yes.

We jumped in, with Gary in the front seat and me in the back with our backpacks and the driver's luggage.

It was claustrophobic back there, and I had no room to move.

As we began driving, the driver told us his story. His wife was divorcing him and taking the children, and he had to get back fast so he could appear in court and fight the decision.

He was also drinking.

He asked if Gary wanted to drive, and Gary, thankfully, said yes.

As we drove through the mountainous, curving roads, it soon became apparent to me that the car had only one working headlight. It also became frighteningly apparent that the guy's brakes were not good at all. This made the mountain drive extremely hairy, to say the least.

I held on in the back with a raging, claustrophobic fear of crashing off the mountain roads for a good six hours. This was probably my first experience with panic attacks, because I had several of them in the back of that Mustang.

It was about all I could take by the time we pulled into Salt Lake City.

We just happened to be dropped off within sight of the Great Salt Lake. As we walked down a dirt road toward the lake, we witnessed what looked like a car chase. Police were chasing a car down the road, sirens blaring, dust flying, and what sounded like gunfire.

We walked in the opposite direction, of course, toward the lake, thinking we were lucky not to have been caught in the crossfire.

As we later found out from a store clerk, they were filming a movie in the area.

We did jump into the Great Salt Lake, and it is true: it is extremely salty. We floated around and swam a little. When we came out, we were covered in a white, salty residue that was not pleasant. We found a water spigot nearby at a shelter house and washed ourselves off.

Then we walked quite a ways back to the highway and stuck out our thumbs for the next ride.

We were stranded for hours.

Apparently, the good folks of Utah believe you should complete your journey the way you started it—and in this case, that meant walking.

So, we began walking, if only to pass the time. At one point, we were attacked by a swarm of flying ants and ran down the side of the highway, swatting at them in a crazed frenzy. As you might imagine, this did not help our chances of being picked up.

We were in the desert now, and needless to say, it was freaking hot. We had very little water and could not seem to get a ride.

Finally, two guys in a pickup truck stopped. They told us they were going to L.A. and would take us all the way if we contributed toward gas money.

We agreed.

There was, however, a serious problem regarding where we were going to ride. The pickup was a standard pickup, so there was no room in the cab. The bed of the truck was covered with a piece of plywood.

The only place for us to ride was on top of the plywood.

There were two large bolts sticking out of it near the cab, so we climbed up and held onto those bolts for dear life, roasting in the sun for hours.

I shouldn't be alive today.

I should have fallen off that truck several times during that ten-hour ride. Somehow, we didn't. When we got into L.A., we were baked, toasted, and severely sunburned.

Through a series of smaller rides, we navigated our way to a hotel just north of Santa Monica, where we rested for a day. We spent the last part of the day swimming in the Pacific, feeling as if we had conquered the world.

Later that evening, we had a great dinner of California hamburgers with avocado and all the fixings. Unfortunately, I got deathly ill that night and threw up for hours. Food poisoning, no doubt. Although Gary had no ill effects, I was just the lucky one, I guess.

I recovered the next day, and we set out to hitchhike up scenic Highway 1 to Malibu. It was a beautiful ride, with great scenery and fantastic views of the Pacific. We camped on a beach for a few days, enjoying the scenery, swimming, and hanging out.

Camping by the ocean is a very moist camping experience. I don't recommend it.

We did not have the proper gear for it, but we were able to dry out our sleeping bags every day in preparation for the next damp night of camping.

At this point, we were running out of cash and needed to head back. We headed back down Route 1 and caught a ride with an interesting gentleman driving an aqua-blue Cordoba. He was very nice and offered to let us stay at his house for the day and enjoy his pool and hot tub.

I was a little apprehensive, but Gary immediately piped up with an enthusiastic, "Yes!"

We must have been in Beverly Hills or some other very wealthy neighborhood, because we pulled up to a beautiful California mansion. As we walked into the house, there was a long hallway lined with pictures of famous movie stars, none of whom I can remember now.

The man was very proud of knowing these people and boasted about all the famous actors he knew as he showed us to the pool and hot tub in the backyard.

He brought out two bottles of champagne and offered us some, which we gladly accepted. Then he proceeded to get completely naked and climb into the hot tub.

For some reason, I had a feeling this was coming. I'm pretty sure he had something in mind when he picked us up.

Gary took off all his clothes and got in, but I kept on my underwear, just to be safe. The man began talking about sex with men and became affectionate toward Gary, but Gary had no intention of letting anything happen. We talked respectfully, but made it clear we were not interested in what he was offering.

We left pretty soon after that. Once he realized we weren't interested, he still kindly dropped us off at a good highway interchange where we could catch a ride heading east out of L.A. We thanked him for his generosity and said goodbye.

We were both heavily buzzed from the champagne and in good moods because of it.

We managed to catch rides out of California, though to be honest, I don't remember many of them. I do remember being stuck outside Las Vegas for many hours. At one point, I laid out my sleeping bag literally five feet from the shoulder of the highway and tried to sleep, but couldn't because of the semi-trucks roaring past. Dangerous and stupid to say the least.

I didn't sleep at all. I should have died that night.

Somehow, we made it to Boulder, Colorado, where we stayed with Gary's brother for a few days. His brother owned a Dairy Queen in Boulder and was doing pretty well, so we stayed in the basement of his condo. I got the feeling he wasn't too happy about us being there, but we were desperate for a warm, dry place to sleep and a shower.

Gary's brother had a party one night, and I remember having a good time—so much so that I passed out in the backyard and didn't remember a thing the next morning.

That was the only time in my life I ever did that.

I am not a great drinker by any means. Never have been, never will be. I did not get that gene from my father, who could drink without much visible effect. Instead, I got my mother's intolerance for alcohol. Probably a good thing.

Our journey from Boulder back to Des Moines was uneventful. We arrived on the outskirts of Des Moines a few days later, where my parents picked us up and delivered us both back to our comfortable homes.

I was glad to see my own bed.

I slept for what seemed like days, and my parents took a picture of me sleeping. I think they wanted to document the safe return of their only son.

To be sure, we were extremely fortunate to make it back relatively unscathed. We were completely oblivious to the possibility of danger, but somehow avoided it. I only wish I could better remember all the conversations we had with the people who picked us up.

We were almost always pleasantly surprised by them. Our rides represented a whole swath of Americana: the whiskey-drinking man who first picked us up, the desperate man trying to get back to fight for his children, the traveling construction workers, and the lonely man in California looking for something we were not willing to give.

Hitchhiking is intrinsically dangerous, for sure, but we were never afraid.

The only thing we were afraid of was not being picked up.

It was an adventure without much planning or thought, but I felt as though it was an accomplishment, the fulfillment of a dream I had carried through much of my teenage life.

College Days and Random Part 1

"Education is an admirable thing, but it is well to remember from time to time that nothing that is worth knowing can be taught."

-Oscar Wilde

I started college in the fall of 1978 at a two-year junior college called Grand View in Des Moines. I had applied to the major Iowa colleges but was not accepted because of my poor grades.

I remember my parents taking me to Iowa State University for some kind of test to determine what subjects I might be interested in. I distinctly remember the man coming out with my results and saying something to the effect of, "You have no strong interest in any area."

Hmmm.

While this felt like a defeat at the time, I think it summed me up in a nutshell. I had broad interests in many things, but no strong interest in any one thing. I suppose I was somewhat of a Renaissance man, if you will.

Such was my fate.

My only strong interest was music. I wanted to study it, but I had no idea what kind of career path I could take from such a major. All I knew was that I loved music and loved playing the guitar.

I did not know how to read music by sight the way trained musicians do. I learned completely by ear, teaching myself songs by listening to them and playing along.

At the time, my parents were moving to Indiana for my dad's new job. I later found out that he had been forced out of his pastor position at the church in Des Moines by deacons who wanted him gone. For what reasons, I do not know. Perhaps his manic states got him into trouble. Or maybe it was his drinking.

He didn't talk about it much, but I do know that his time at First Presbyterian Church in Des Moines was, at the very least, bumpy.

He kept a flask of bourbon in his car, along with a spray bottle of Listerine. I only know this because I occasionally drove his car and discovered the flask while looking for something I had dropped under the seat.

Looking back on that time, I can recognize when my dad was either manic or depressed. But to me, back then, it mostly seemed normal.

Needless to say, it was not.

I loved my life at Grand View College.

Going to classes like Music Theory and Music Composition was interesting and challenging. I was also taking voice, piano, and classical guitar, as well as singing in the Grand View Choir, which was quite good at the time.

Because my parents had moved to Indiana, I was living in the dorm. It was there that I met Jim, a strange and somewhat disgruntled misfit who played guitar like no one I had ever met before. Jim was distantly related to Gene Autry, the famous country music star, but his own musical taste was eclectic and centered mostly around Frank Zappa.

Jim and I played guitar together and eventually formed a band. My good friend Lumpy was the drummer, and Bob, a fellow music student, played bass. We had no singer, so I did all the singing—and not very well, at least at first. I got better as we went on.

We worked up a couple of sets and played a few gigs at friends' parties. In 1978, Grand View had a substantial Iranian student population due to the civil unrest in Iran and the eventual overthrow of the 2,500-year-old monarchy. The lead-up to the Iranian Revolution was a dangerous time for many citizens, and the eventual establishment of the Islamic Republic under Grand Ayatollah Khomeini forced many people to leave.

Amazingly enough, some of those Iranian students landed smack dab in the middle of Iowa, at Grand View College.

I became friends with some of them, and when they were looking for a band to play at the college-sponsored Iranian New Year's party, I offered up my band, now known as The Fake Babies, for the gig.

They naively accepted, not knowing we had only about twelve songs under our belt and would be hard-pressed to play for two hours.

As it turned out, the college paid us $600 to play, which was unheard of for local bands at the time. We played the gig in the basement of the women's dorm, and it was a strange spectacle, to say the least.

We played several Led Zeppelin songs, including one with a twenty-minute drum solo, along with a garbled, mediocre version of "Stairway to Heaven," a few Elvis Costello songs, and several others I can no longer remember. Much of the crowd disappeared after our first set. I don't think they were too pleased with our performance, but we never heard any complaints and didn't make any enemies.

Perhaps a bit of revenge occurred when the dorm cafeteria agreed to let the Iranian students prepare traditional food for dinner. The night after that meal, I became deathly ill with severe dry heaves, fever, and the general feeling that I was dying.

The next day, a friend drove me to the doctor, where I was diagnosed with hepatitis. I was promptly admitted to the hospital and quarantined for a week, until I was able to function again.

I doubt it was the food that got me.

Maybe it was karma.

After that gig, we somehow miraculously landed another one: playing the Ankeny High School spring prom for the amazing sum of $800. We learned a few more songs for this performance, but again had to repeat many of them throughout the night.

Those suburban kids did not enjoy their spring prom dance very much, but I didn't feel bad about it one bit. In fact, I despised the suburban blight of Ankeny. It was a place of strip malls, thousands of look-alike houses, rows of condos and townhomes, and, in my opinion, soulless suburbia.

Ironically, those two gigs were the highest-paid performances of my entire musical career.

The money was all downhill from there on out.

But the music got much better.

I did well academically at Grand View.

Very well, in fact.

I graduated with an associate degree in music.

Very useful indeed.

I then decided to enroll at the University of Iowa in their music department. In order to do so, I had to take a series of incredibly difficult entrance exams, which I failed miserably because of my lack of formal music training.

Somehow, I decided instead to major in political science and minor in philosophy—two subjects that in no way prepared me for work in the real world.

But I sometimes believe that, for many people, including me, college is a place to find out what you don't want to do.

I was never fortunate enough to have a single path, a single passion, or a clear road toward a chosen career. Nor did I aspire to make lots of money. I was, instead, a student of life.

I had many different interests and talents, but no idea what I wanted to do for a living.

So, after graduating with a bachelor's degree in political science, I floundered.

I drifted.

I struggled.

My long-term girlfriend, Jani, went to the University of Iowa a year before I did. I used to hitchhike up there on weekends to visit her.

When I finally moved to Iowa City, we lived next door to each other, fooling our parents into thinking we weren't living together, when in fact, for all practical purposes, we were.

Unlike me, Jani got a good job right out of college working for the IRS. I, with my major in political science and minor in philosophy, could not find a decent job. That, coupled with my desire to play music in a rock-and-roll band, led to our eventual breakup.

Maybe breakup is the wrong word to use in this case. We decided to take a break from each other. But during this break, she met another dude and slept with him. This devastated me for a good long while.

We had been together for seven long years. We were going to get married, buy a house, and probably have children. Ironically, all of the things I later found abhorrent. The whole nine yards. I struggled with depression and thoughts of suicide. I had trouble imagining life without her, it was rough going. To make things worse I was poor, barely getting by with rent and food. Life after college did not have the desired results I was hoping for.

I had a crappy job making four dollars an hour at Younkers Warehouse, a local department store. This left me with very few options to afford living. As a result, I lived in some pretty awful places. At one point, I lived in an efficiency apartment off University Avenue and 21st Street, just down from the funeral home and the car wash. It was a dangerous and impoverished neighborhood, known at the time for crime and violence. Ten years later, the infamous 1992 Drake Diner murders took place just blocks from my apartment. That crime has never been solved.

There was no air conditioning in that apartment. I tried to sleep with the windows open, but the sounds from the neighborhood frightened me. There were occasional gunshots, people shouting and screaming. The neighbors upstairs fought constantly and had loud, violent sex.

So, I closed my windows at night and slept with a fan blowing air out of the open refrigerator.

It was miserable.

My car was vandalized almost every night, even though I left it unlocked in the hope that nothing would get damaged. There was nothing to steal from my 1970 yellow VW Bug, which I had received as a college graduation present. It had a four-speed clutch, an engine in the back, little to no heat or defrost, and a few rust spots around the fenders and running boards.

It cost $800 in 1982, and somehow, it remained a reliable car for four years.

I'm sure you know that the VW Bug was designed by Ferdinand Porsche, with the help of none other than Adolf Hitler. Volkswagen was once a state-owned car company, and the Bug was Hitler's pet project: an affordable but speedy vehicle for the masses.

Who knew the hippie Bug had a Nazi connection?

There were mice in the apartment. They would chew holes right through my loaves of bread, bag and all. Nothing was safe unless it was stored in the refrigerator.

At one point, a mouse must have died in my closet, because when I opened the door one day, a swarm of flying insects came out.

The place sucked.

Things were pretty bleak.

Changes had to be made.

As it turned out, the breakup with Jani was a major fork in the road for me. From disaster came opportunities, musically, academically, professionally and so much more. I would meet so many interesting people that I would never have met had I continued my life with Jani. Some of these people had a profound influence on my life. And yet, had Jani and I married who knows. Random ambiguity strikes again!

Many years later, I found out that Jani had slept with my best friend, Lumpy. Unknowingly, I returned the favor soon after by sleeping with his long-term girlfriend. Lumpy and I both laughed about this irony over a couple of beers. Strangely enough, it did not affect our friendship at all.

After living in poverty for so long, I eventually made the decision to go back to school and enroll in a paralegal program at a local community college called DMACC. My parents generously offered to help with tuition, and they paid for me to live in a decent efficiency apartment while I attended school.

I was, indeed, a fortunate son.

My parents rescued me, as they would do several times in my early adult life. Had they not been there to help me, I'm not sure where I would be today.

I did well in the paralegal program, and I enjoyed it.

At the same time, I was playing in a cover band and performing regularly. I was meeting lots of girls, though none I was especially interested in. Besides, I didn't have the courage to talk to the pretty ones.

One of the highlights of my early musical career was playing gigs at a small club called So's Your Mother. This club was the center of alternative music in Des Moines and served as a place where local alternative music could grow and find an audience.

If you got a gig there, it was a big deal.

Locally and nationally known bands played there, including Hüsker Dü and the Violent Femmes. I saw the Violent Femmes show there.

It was also, incidentally, the last place a twenty-year-old woman named Diane Schofield was seen before she was murdered. The case was never solved and was almost featured on the show *Cold Justice*. Schofield was later found in the trunk of her car in a southside parking lot. Robbery was ruled out as a motive, and the case remains an Iowa cold case.

It is strange to think I may have been there that night.

Anyway, it was at this club that I met a girl named Mia. We immediately hit it off, and I found her very easy to talk to. We were strongly attracted to each other and became entangled for a couple of years.

She was intelligent, artistic, pretty, and outspoken.

And, while this may seem inappropriate to mention, she was also a virgin.

She exposed me to great music, film, literature, and other things. She attended school at the University of Iowa but was home for the summer. We maintained our relationship while she was at the university, and I would travel up to stay with her on weekends.

We went on a few adventures together, including driving to New York City and attending a U2 concert in Cleveland along the way.

It was around this time that I became frustrated with my band. We were playing cover songs but not writing our own material. I considered giving up the guitar altogether and getting a real job that actually paid.

I also remember seeing the movie *Harold and Maude* at Mia's suggestion, and it affected me greatly. I still consider it one of the truly great film-and-soundtrack combinations of all time. Life and death, old and young, love and loss—these are some of the themes of that great movie.

Great films change you forever. They make you think and feel things in ways you cannot easily explain. Words are hard to come by when trying to describe *Harold and Maude.* Though it is often called a dark comedy, it is also a tragic and beautiful story, one you have to see and experience for yourself. The scene with the priest and Harold remains, in my opinion, one of the funniest monologues in cinematic history.

A severely cold Iowa winter, the slow and mutual breakup with Mia, and the fizzling out of my band all came together to make this a dark time for me.

And yet, it is a time I still relish.

I was not devastated by the breakup. From the very beginning, I had the sense that I was a stepping stone for her—a rock-and-roll guitarist who served a certain purpose in her life. But for me, she was an awakening.

Needless to say, I never became a paralegal.

Opportunity missed.

Fork in the road.

That could have been a lucrative career. Instead, I happened upon a part-time job at a medical insurance company, which eventually turned into a ten-year gig paying medical claims.

It was during this time that I formed my first original band.

Writing and playing original music was much more fun and rewarding than playing covers. We were creating and performing regularly. We recorded some songs in a studio and were included on an album called *The Iowa Compilation.* We also traveled to Madison, Wisconsin, to record in a real professional recording studio.

We had hopes of being discovered by a producer.

But it never happened.

There are moments when I wish I could simply cease to exist.

I want this anxiety and depression to end. Is this how I am going to feel for the rest of my life? I can't take this anymore.

Yesterday, I jokingly told my wife that it's a damn good thing I have anxiety, otherwise I would never get out of bed. I laughed when I said it, but she did not find it amusing.

I'm not sure how much I should share with her about the way I'm feeling. I don't want to burden her or make her anxious, too. We do not need both of us feeling this way.

I don't feel good. I never feel good about anything. I want to feel good about my life. I know I have a lot to feel good about, but I can't seem to get there.

When I wake up, I get my son up, make his lunch, and stay on top of him to get ready for school. Then I drive him there. All the while, I just want to go back to bed.

Sometimes I do.

But there is no sleep to be found. The anxiety kicks in, and then I am left forcing myself to deal with the daily tasks of family management, survival, and trying not to spiral out of control.

Sometimes I drive for Uber. Sometimes I work for the Post Office. I worry about money. I worry about the future of our family. I worry about everything.

Anxiety has become my mind's default setting. It feels like a habit, a trained response that happens every single day.

I know that you probably don't understand this. I didn't understand it until I contracted this horrible disease. Unless you have felt severe anxiety, you cannot understand it. You will not understand it. Period.

I know this all too well because I watched my mother experience debilitating anxiety. She suffered greatly from what looked to me, at the time, like pointless worrying. Infinite worrying. Endless self-doubt.

I could not, for the life of me, understand it then. To me, it seemed simple: stop worrying, let it go, things will be all right, people love you, people will take care of you.

I did not have as much compassion for her as I should have because I thought she could simply stop it.

I feel terrible about that now.

I regret not being more understanding. I hate myself for it. Why didn't I help her more? I cried for her and felt horrible for her, but why didn't I try harder to help?

I told myself she could somehow choose not to be anxious.

I know better now.

The Bus and Europe

"We travel, some of us forever, to seek other states, other lives, other souls."
-Anais Nin

Around 1987, I decided to trade my 1984 VW Rabbit for a 1970 VW camper bus, my dream vehicle. It had a pop-up roof with a cot for sleeping. The back featured a bed, a sitting area with a table, a refrigerator, and a sink. It was a place where I could live and travel. My vision of a nomadic, self-contained life was taking shape.

At the same time, I had no clue what to do with my life. I was working for a health insurance company, making good money, but I hated it. So, I quit, cashed in my savings, and planned to travel to Europe with friends. I was 27. What the hell, why not?

I drove the bus across the country to my parents, then up to my sister's in Pennsylvania. I would leave it there until I returned from Europe. If I returned.

Band mates Charles and Dave were my traveling companions for this adventure, at least for some of the trip. We had gotten our passports and had purchased EurRail passes to ride the trains throughout the countries of Europe for eight weeks. We all had our flight booked to London out of New York. It was a one-way ticket. There were no solid plans to come back, other than when our money ran out. We were planning on staying in youth hostels or a bed and breakfast because they were cheap. We were flying by the seat of our pants. I took the train from Doylestown, Pennsylvania to New York to meet Dave and Charles. They had flown out from Des Moines. Somehow, we managed to get together and found a place to stay at my old girlfriend Mia's tiny apartment in Brooklyn. We all had our backpacks and had a few days to kill in New York. I don't remember much about those few days other than securing visas, getting some British currency and purchasing our EurRail passes. I do remember one incident while going to a coffee shop with my friend. I went into the shop and got tired of waiting for my friend to do whatever it was she was doing so I went outside to wait. As I stood up against a wall this freaked out junkie looking guy came up to me, got up in my face and said these exact words, "I know you, you're that bitch from the train the other day, I should cut your fucking throat right here." I froze speechless not knowing whether to run or get ready to defend myself against a knife attack. Then, this crazy dude just walked away, like nothing ever happened. I was a little freaked out after that, and I will never forget that encounter for the rest of my life.

We flew out of New York late at night and arrived at London's Heathrow Airport around 11:00 a.m. Just standing there felt like stepping back in time—

I can't explain it, but it was as if I was standing on thousands of years of history.

We found a cheap hotel tucked among a row of houses. It had three beds, a bathroom down the hall, breakfast in the morning, and access to a kitchen. We stayed for about five days, exploring London: art museums, Piccadilly Square, Hyde Park, and the pubs. Mostly, we just wandered.

One night we discovered a farmer's market, bought some food, and cooked dinner. We didn't eat much; breakfast was the important meal because it was free. It was terrible—baked beans, stewed tomatoes, toast, and tea—but free. Each morning, a group of loud Scottish men would gather, speaking in thick accents. We rarely understood them and never knew if they were reminiscing about their drunken night or plotting to beat us up and take our money.

Dave and I left England the same day, heading for Ireland via the Pembrokeshire Coast of Wales, while Charles went on to Brighton. We boarded a train to Fishguard, planning to hike the coast before catching a ferry.

We arrived in Fishguard in pouring rain and found a bed-and-breakfast about a mile uphill from the station. We were soaked by the time we got there, but the home turned out to be charming: two beds, a small television, a view of the harbor, and the all-important included breakfast. I remember that sense of warmth and comfort, sitting on the bed and looking out over the harbor on a rainy afternoon. The house seemed steeped in history—centuries of lives and dreams, countless others staring out this window, perhaps imagining travel to distant lands.

After changing into dry clothes, we explored. Wales was everything I'd imagined: historic castles, rolling green hills, sheer cliffs dropping into the sea, and quaint harbor villages. The rain had stopped, letting us wander into the countryside along a hiking trail. On the way back, we grabbed takeout and relaxed in our warm beds, watching *10* with Bo Derek on the tiny TV—surprised the film hadn't been censored like it would be in the U.S.

The next morning, we packed our backpacks and tackled the Pembrokeshire Coastal Trail. It was bloody windy, wet, and cold, but the scenery was breathtaking. The 12-mile hike was grueling—up and down steep paths, green pastures on one side, dramatic sea cliffs on the other. Massive rock formations jutted into the sea, and we hiked right to the edges, the wind threatening to blow us off.

After a couple of hours, we stumbled back to Fishguard for a pint, then headed back up the trail in search of a campsite. We found an abandoned building with broken walls and no roof and ate dinner: canned mackerel in tomato sauce, peanuts, raisins, orange juice, and rice cakes. Camping was impossible—the wind and drizzle were relentless, and we were ill-prepared.

We hiked back to the dock and waited for the 3 a.m. ferry across the Irish Sea to Roslare, Ireland. A footnote: the 1956 classic film *Moby Dick* was partially filmed in Fishguard.

The ferry was massive.... a parking-garage-sized behemoth, cars lined up to enter the bottom deck. Dave and I boarded onto the main deck, which had a bar, restaurant, public seating, and a separate, more expensive area with recliner-type chairs. There were also two outside decks, but it was cold and raining, so we stayed inside.

As soon as the ship left port, I realized this crossing was going to be rough. The back-and-forth motion made me nauseous immediately. I fell asleep for a bit, only to be jerked awake, thrown partially out of my chair. Dave looked as sick as I felt, and we both had the overwhelming urge to vomit. It became every man for himself.

I staggered to the back window to see waves crashing over the stern. Around me, people were vomiting wherever they stood or sat. The ship was thrashing so violently it felt like a funhouse ride at the state fair. I tried to reach the bathroom, bouncing off walls to maintain balance, only to discover utter chaos: vomit coating walls, floors, cigarette receptacles, and garbage cans. Every sink and toilet was occupied by people convulsing violently.

I stumbled back out, found a clean spot on the floor, and laid flat on my back, fighting the urge to throw up. Somehow, I survived. Hours later, as the ship docked, the captain announced over the intercom that it had been "the worst crossing of his career"—and I believed him.

Dazed and confused Dave and I exited the ferry into Roslare, Ireland, utterly spent. We found a bed-and-breakfast in Wexford and slept for what felt like days. Breakfast was surprisingly good, though I can't recall the details. Simply being alive felt incredible.

We took a bus to Dublin and spent the day walking, but I began feeling ill—an upper respiratory issue and fever. We checked into a hostel—a single large room with 20–25 squeaky bunk beds. Snoring and creaking created a nightmarish symphony; sleep was minimal. Germans arrived late, loud in their language, and in my half-asleep state, it frightened me.

The next day we took a train back to Roslare and stayed at a much nicer hostel, finally getting the rest we desperately needed. This was critical, because we were about to board another ferry, a 17-hour crossing to Cherbourg, France.

Mercifully, this ferry crossing wasn't nearly as rough, though 17 hours still felt brutal, especially since I felt awful. Cherbourg was a shady port town, and finding a place to stay proved difficult. A couple of local guys offered to take us to a hotel with openings. We were apprehensive, expecting a scam, but they turned out honest and helpful.

The hotel was cheap, dirty, and noisy, with bright neon lights flashing all night. Sleep was impossible; my cough kept me awake. The next day I bought cough drops at a local drugstore, and we boarded a train to Lisbon, Portugal, via Madrid. Before leaving, we left a message on the station's bulletin board for Charles, letting him know we were heading to Portugal.

We chose Portugal because it was an overnight train ride, saving money on accommodations, and it sounded appealing: warm, by the ocean. The train started off crowded, and we were riding… shoulder to shoulder with four other passengers in a hot sweaty passenger car with no air-conditioning. It was 2nd class. Unfortunately for me I did not realize that because of my age and EurRail Pass I could travel in first class. I found this out at the border of France and Spain and was delighted that I had a passenger car all to myself with cushioned bench seats that folded into beds and cabin doors that could be made private with a glass door and curtains. I felt bad for Dave, but it didn't last long as I drifted to sleep in my private cabin.

We arrived in Madrid and, low and behold, there was Charles leaning against a handrail at the station. We spent some time exploring the Moors Palace and sitting by a small lake with boats and a fountain. I took a picture of myself there; looking back, I appear strung out, gaunt from hunger, but somewhat relieved to feel the warmth of the sun.

Portugal was indeed warm and welcoming. In Lisbon, we met two guys and a girl catching the next train to Cascais. They said it was nicer and cheaper than Lisbon, so we followed them, sharing stories as we walked. Each of us found a bed-and-breakfast and agreed to meet later at the small harbor, filled with brightly colored fishing boats.

Our bed-and-breakfast was beautiful and comfortable. I even took a picture of the front of the building—now a large portrait on my dining room wall. We rested, then met our new friends at the harbor with a couple of bottles of port wine, Portugal's specialty. We drank and watched the sun sink into the ocean.

We stayed in Cascais for a few days. On our last evening, we went to a small restaurant owned by a woman who had been a nanny in California. She was kind and brought pitchers of wine, escargot, and bread for free. We bought a small plate of swordfish steak and shared it—it was the best meal I'd had in weeks.

The girl we had met, Lena, was part Indian and part Scandinavian; her father lived in D.C., her mother in France. She asked to travel with us, tired of her two companions. We agreed, and next we headed off to Barcelona, Spain.

The train pulled into Badajoz, Spain, a small town just across the border from Portugal. We had to switch trains here to continue on to Barcelona. When we exited the train and walked into the station, we were all a little groggy. We did not expect to go through a station security check before boarding our next train.

At first, things seemed to move quickly, until Charles was asked to empty his backpack. As he began pulling out baggies of vitamins and green herbal supplements that looked a little like weed, I realized we were in serious trouble. The security officer spoke no English, we spoke no Spanish, and the confusion only made everything worse.

We were all motioned into a separate security area while they went through our belongings. None of us had anything suspicious.... except Charles. We sat there for hours, not knowing what was going on, until a police car arrived with lights flashing and siren blaring. *What the devil is this? Are we going to jail? This is bad, very bad,* I thought.

Two men and a woman, dressed very professionally, entered the room. We tried to communicate that Charles's items were just vitamins and supplements, but they insisted on taking each of us to a back room for a strip search. It was terrifying. Thank God they didn't perform a cavity search. Of course, they found nothing.

When it was all over, I tried to take a picture of the officers, but they looked very unreceptive, so I didn't push it. By this time, we had missed our train to Barcelona and were forced to spend many more hours in Badajoz waiting for the next one. The only thing I remember about Badajoz were the swallows, who had made mud nests underneath a bridge we crossed. That's it.

In Barcelona, we wandered around for a while, but the city felt overwhelmingly large at that moment. We grabbed something to eat and caught the next train to Nice, France. The ride was scenic, with the Mediterranean glimmering alongside the tracks. We passed through Marseille and other picturesque coastal towns before arriving in Nice.

We found a spacious but sparse room with four beds and a bathroom down the hall, where you had to pay for a shower by the minute. Nice was a total beach vacation: warm, restorative, and a welcome break from the relentless train travel.

We got to know Lena, she was intelligent, honest, funny and easy to hang out with. One night, she and I went swimming in the Mediterranean. It was hard not to swim to her and embrace. Afterward we walked back to the hotel shivering from the cool night air. I gave her my shirt. I wanted to hold her hand, I wanted to kiss her. *There was something there, something... or maybe it was just me.* I'll never really know. She was very beautiful. Ambiguity...

We stayed in touch after Europe. In fact, I used Lena's artwork on the cover of my first solo recording, a cassette tape called *Sex and Love*, which I gave away to about ten people.

After Nice, we all split up, heading to different countries. I decided to travel to Salzburg, Austria, via Innsbruck. In Salzburg, I stayed several days in a beautiful mountain-valley bed and breakfast. I hiked the nearby trails, visited Mozart's boyhood home, and absorbed the music that seemed to inhabit every corner of the city. Street musicians were everywhere, classical quartets, jazz ensembles, even a South American panpipe player. Music was inescapable.

Tourists were also everywhere. I survived on a mix of careful budgeting and opportunism: buying a loaf of bread and water, occasionally splurging on cheese or meat, and scavenging abandoned food left on patio tables—an uneaten roll here, a stray piece of fruit there. Money was tight, and I adapted. I asked strangers for cigarettes and, in tougher moments, grabbed a few from ashtrays. Survival required improvisation, and I became a resourceful opportunist.

From Austria, I traveled briefly to Switzerland, taking a scenic train ride to Spiez, a mountain-lake town. I spent the day swimming in Lake Thun and lounging in the sun. The place was pristine, almost too perfect. I spoke to no one and met no fellow travelers; it was obvious to many that I was an unkempt outsider.

That evening, I caught the night train to Amsterdam, where I would spend a few days before continuing to Paris to catch my flight back to New York.

I arrived in Amsterdam and found a room in a bed-and-breakfast above a restaurant. I shared it with a scary, unhinged American who was desperate to get back to the States. He terrified me…I feared he would rob me blind if I left anything in the room, so I locked my valuables at the train station and carried only what I needed for a few days in the city.

The room was large, with several bunk beds. I took the top bunk farthest from him. Our only conversation was about his desperate desire to return to the U.S., but not having enough money. He asked me for money; I explained I barely had enough to get home myself. After that, he began muttering to himself in a strange, disturbing way that made me want to leave the room immediately.

I set out to explore Amsterdam.

Walking around Amsterdam was somewhat disturbing for me, as one of the first things I saw was a homeless man taking a shit in broad daylight in plain sight of all. Yet no one seemed to notice but me. People were walking by as if it were another day in Amsterdam. It just so happened that he was doing his business right next to a pornography store, of which there seemed to be a lot in Amsterdam. I moved on.

I searched for and found the hiding place of Anne Frank and her family during the Nazi invasion. It was eerie and unsettling for me to be near it, to actually be there where her family hid from horror and almost made it. Almost… I then moved on to the Van Gogh Museum, where nearly half of his work is displayed: early sketches, *Sunflowers*, *Bedroom in Arles*, *Wheat Fields with Crows*, *Irises*, and self-portraits. I am a big fan of Van Gogh, so I was awe-struck to be in the same room with these paintings. *Van Gogh, Anne Frank, is it normal to want to seek out tragically themed historical places? I can't help but question myself.*

After wandering a bit more along the canals, I stumbled onto a farmer's market and ate some beets, bread, and salted fish of some sort. It was now time to explore the bars of Amsterdam and the infamous marijuana freedom. I visited my first bar and sat down to have a beer. I really don't like Heineken…it is a skunky-tasting beer in my opinion, but I drank it anyway. At the bar, they were passing around joints filled with weed and tobacco, which made no sense to me. Hitting hard on tobacco even with the weed made me feel really awful. I looked over the weed menu and went over to the little weed bar and bought a small amount for later, thinking that I would be smoking more during my stay.

But as I walked through the streets of Amsterdam, on the bridges over the many canals, back to my scary hostel room with the crazy man waiting for me, I began to feel sick. Not just physically, but emotionally as well. I was not enjoying this high. As I passed some kids on the bridge, I asked them if they wanted some weed. They laughed at me, like I was unaware that they could get weed anywhere and probably already had some, and that this was not how weed was dealt in Amsterdam. I clarified and said, "No, I mean do you want some free weed that I just bought over at the bar, I don't want it." They said sure, somewhat in disbelief, and I felt somewhat untethered and a little freed up from that burden.

I made it back to my hostel room and laid down on my bunk, immediately experiencing the worst spins in my life. I was also afraid to sleep because I thought the crazy guy was going to slit my throat and take my locker key to the train station locker where all of my stuff was. The first time I had to puke, I made it to the bathroom down the hall and violently let go of the evil inside. It was pure beet red coming out, which was a little scary at first. I remembered that I had eaten a bunch of beets and felt a little better. I made my way back to the room, lay down for another few minutes, but had to puke again, and this time there was no making it to the bathroom. I climbed out the window of the room onto the fire escape balcony, bent over the rail, and let it go. It was violent and grotesque. As I was puking, I heard the tiny sound of metal tinkling off…

The key had fallen to the side of the railing and onto the fire escape balconies below. It was my locker key—the key to the train station locker where my passport, money, and all my belongings were safe and secure. Fuck! Fuck, Fuck, Fuck! I had to get it back.

I began climbing down the fire escape ladder, dizzy, heaving vomit as I went, stopping on each balcony to look for the key to my existence. Miracle upon miracle, I saw it. Somehow it had not fallen through the fire escape to the alley below and was precariously sitting on the third balcony below mine. I climbed down, heaved more vomit until I reached it, grabbed the key, and climbed back up, vomiting the whole way. Phew!

I collapsed into my bunk and lay awake all night. Fortunately, there was no more puking, but that crazy dude was still 20 feet away. I was determined to make it through the night.

The next morning, I ate my free breakfast, checked out, and wandered along the canals a bit. After a short nap, I headed back to the train station to retrieve my belongings. There, who did I see? Dave in his usual dull blue flannel shirt and grey Chuck Taylors. We caught up on each other's travels, and then he pointed out the Krishna van giving away free vegetable curry. I asked if it was any good (I didn't want to get sick again), and he said it was great. As I approached the line, there was Charles sitting on a bench eating his meal.

I got my food and donated what little Guilders I had left. It tasted incredible, and I was grateful for the free meal, as money was running dangerously low. Dave and Charles had rented bikes, so I jumped on the back of Dave's, and we rode around Amsterdam and out into the countryside.

My experience in Amsterdam had been, at best, interesting, but mostly it felt dangerous and unpleasant. I decided it was time to go home—I'd had enough and was ready to find comfort and familiarity with family and friends. Money was almost gone, too. I boarded the train to Paris, where my flight was in two days back to New York. I planned to meet the boys and Lena for one last night together.

On this last train from Amsterdam to Paris, someone thought it would be funny to run down the aisle yelling, "Oh my God, there's a bomb on the train!" For one split second, I felt an incredible panic and horror, stood up, and opened the cabin door to run. But then I realized that if there really was a bomb, there was nowhere to run and nothing I could do. The other passengers in my cabin reacted the same way. We all gave ourselves up to the inevitable, wishing we could get our hands on the bastard. It wasn't funny at all.

I arrived early in the morning, two days before my flight, and met everyone at the train station. We walked the streets of Paris: the Eiffel Tower, the Champs-Élysées, the Arc de Triomphe, Notre Dame Cathedral, and the Louvre.

At Notre Dame, I heard an organ recital that was utterly ethereal. The sun shone through the stained-glass windows, the organ notes resounded and shook the very ground—it felt unearthly. I'll never forget that vibrating sensation.

We wandered through the Louvre, which was overwhelming, but we managed to see the Mona Lisa and a few other masterpieces.

For dinner, we stumbled into a Greek restaurant that was alive with energy. A Greek trio sang and played while people danced in the aisles. There were no standard dining tables, everyone sat at long picnic-style tables, drinking, eating, singing, and dancing. The owner, I think, walked around sharing shots of Sambuca and smashing the glasses against the fireplace wall, yelling "Oupa!" each time. For a moment, I wondered if we had wandered into a private party, but nobody seemed to care that we were there.

I don't even remember where I slept that night. I think it was the train station, but I have no memory of it. I do remember saying good-bye to everyone and giving Lena a long embrace in which I had an enormous boner and felt embarrassed about. Hey, it had been six weeks since anything had happened down there. Which reminds me of a really funny story Dave told me about later after our trip. As it turns out he and Lena had to travel in second class together on the trains in pretty cramped quarters because of their youth. Lena had fallen asleep with her head on Dave's lap. Dave, being 18 and probably easily provoked, uncontrollably ejaculated, had a wet dream while Lena was sleeping on his lap Dave panicked, woke Lena up, went to the bathroom, changed his pants and hoped that no one had noticed. He was pretty sure no one had.

I had about 36 hours to kill before my flight left for New York, so I headed to the airport and decided to camp out there just to make sure I wouldn't miss my flight. As the flight got closer to leaving, I just so happened to go check with the counter about meals on the flight, because I had very little money and was starving. The ticket woman told me that I was at the wrong airport and needed to go to Orly International Airport instead of Charles de Gaulle. She gave me instructions on where to catch a bus to Orly, and I ran out of the airport to the bus depot to catch the next bus. I arrived with little time to spare.

Finding the correct terminal was difficult, as my ticket was with a budget airline, so I had to take a shuttle to an outdoor terminal inside a great big tent. There, I had to wait in line behind the counter of I can't remember what airline. However, I did notice that every single airline seemed Middle Eastern: Air Egypt, Air Jordan, Air Libya, Air Syria, etc., etc. Great, I thought, every fucking airline here is from a nation that hates Americans. A very narrow way of thinking, yes, I know, but I was at the end of my rope and in survival mode. I needed to get on that plane, beg for double dinners, and get the fuck back to America.

As I boarded the plane, I felt some relief, and when I finally sat in my assigned seat, I relaxed a little more. I asked the nice stewardess to bring me an extra dinner if there were any left over, and she did. My belly was full, I was 30,000 feet in the air over the Atlantic Ocean, and I was on my way home. Actually, I didn't really have a home or a plan at that time, but that would come later.

When I arrived in New York it was a little surreal. I took the subway to the train station and got on a train to Doylestown, Pennsylvania where my sister lived. I arrived at about 2 am in the morning. Fortunately, my sister and brother-in-law were gracious enough to pick me up. I slept for days, occasionally getting up to eat something. I was painfully thin and hadn't shaved for two months. After about a week or so of exploring job opportunities in the area where my sister lived, I drove down to see my parents in Wilmington, North Carolina. I was thinking of settling down there and trying to find a job. The old adage, "you can never go home again" comes to mind here. By home I mean living with your parents, because North Carolina was not my home. Living with your parents as an adult is not good! My parents were not getting along very well at this time and each of them took me in as their confidant. There are things that we should not know about our parents I think. My father would talk to me about his frustration with my mother and his affair that he had when they were younger. "If your mother knew about that she would throw me out." My mother would talk to me about how difficult it was to live with a manic depressant and how she just had to go on with her life and live it without my father. Each of them was struggling in their own way and I was caught in the middle.

My father had bought a small sailboat (a Sunfish) and named it *'Ruthless'*, my mother's name was Ruth. He didn't know how to sail very well, but I had had some classes and experiences, so he invited me to go down to the bay and sail with him. My dad seemed to know many of the men that hung out around the dock, and it all seemed like a pretty good thing. One of his buddies took me aside and told me privately that my dad was probably going to end up killing himself. He had already run into some other larger and nicer boats and had had to be rescued a few times by his friends. Anyway, we got the boat ready and took off in the bay. Things went pretty well for a little bit as my dad was giving me bits of advice when he decided to tack with a sharp tiller toward the sail. He fell out of the boat and on I went trying to grab the tiller and the boom before the whole thing tipped over. I got control of the boat, all the while my dad shouting out directions to me which I didn't need. I swung back around and got him back on the boat and we headed back to the dock. We laughed about it quite a bit, and when we told my mother about it she did not find it amusing. She had already been notified by the authorities about my dad's reckless sailing at the bay. Let's just say it was a sore point for her. I lasted a few days longer at my parents' place and then decided to head back to the only thing that resembled a home, Des Moines, Iowa.

The Loneliest Road in America

"In the solitude of solo travel, the mind expands, and the spirit dances to the rhythm of the open road."
-Jack Kerouac

Getting back to Des Moines after staying with my folks in North Carolina was, I must admit, comfortable. I lived in my red VW bus on the streets of Des Moines or stayed with some friends when they offered. My relationship with Moon was practically over, even though she let me stay at her place for a few days. I often look back on this time as the simplest of my life. I had one key to my name, the key to my bus; and everything I owned was in that bus.

It was at this time that my band, 23 Lies, decided to take one last chance at rock and roll. We got it in our heads to go to San Francisco, establish ourselves with some gigs, and get famous, or something like that. Supposedly, we had a place to stay for a while with a friend of Charles'. All of us were ready to go except for our drummer, Lumpy, who was married and had a baby. He thought he would come out later once we got our living situation set up.

We loaded up the bus with Lumpy's drums, our guitars, and amps. The lead singer, Charles, and bass player, Tim, were driving in a separate car with a flaky friend who was not part of the band, and I, of course, drove by myself. I should have known this endeavor was doomed from the beginning, but oh well; it was an adventure, and I was all about the experience. I used to say that the only regrets in life are the chances we don't take, not the ones we do.

We left Des Moines and headed west on Interstate 80. The first night we stopped at a rest stop near Carney, Nebraska. We all grabbed some food and sat at a picnic table. On top of the table was a stack of Polaroid photographs of rather large and unattractive people engaging in sexual activities. On the last picture, there was the name "Carney Swinger's Club" and a phone number. It was a somewhat disturbing discovery and maybe a bad omen for the trip. We laughed about the pictures and the David Lynch-like possibilities and then continued on our way.

The drive to San Francisco was relatively uneventful after that, other than driving through a severe windstorm in Nevada. My spare tire cover got ripped off by the wind and taken to who knows where. Driving a VW bus in serious wind is no picnic due to its shape. I had to physically steer into the wind for many hours just to keep the bus on the road. It was exhausting and nerve-racking.

Finally, we made it to California and pulled off on a country road to rest. I ended up staying there by myself to sleep while Charles, Tim, and company went into town to arrange a place for us to stay. Supposedly, we had a friend we could crash with to get our feet on the ground and get the band started. As it turned out, Charles and Tim could stay with the friend, but there wasn't room for me. Even though I hauled Lumpy's drum set all the way to San Francisco, he never made it. Who could blame him? He had a newborn baby girl and a job. Why would he risk that on a crazy, whimsical, no-plan pipe dream? I was somewhat disappointed, to say the least, but at least I had the bus to sleep in on the streets of San Francisco.

San Francisco is cold as hell in August, especially at night. I was a little lost. I explored Haight-Ashbury, the Golden Gate Bridge and Park, and even played tennis barefoot there. Chinatown, Lombard Street, and endless wandering. I ate free food at the St. John Coltrane Church and at various places around the city, including bagels I found at a dumpster.

I parked my bus with a great view of the Painted Ladies; the famous Victorian houses, right next to a beautiful little park. I would lay down on a blanket there and take naps some days. There were times when I felt a little scared. Some people looked dangerous, and I found myself crossing the street several times to avoid sketchy folks.

My friend Charles (singer and lyricist) was not able to secure a place for me to live, but he did find a place for himself and his sketchy friend. That move left me hanging and feeling a little abandoned. In fact, I saw very little of him or the bass player, Tim, who had also made the trip. I became a little soured on the whole band thing and felt a bit betrayed. I hung out for a week or so, but we never played a song in San Francisco. I started thinking about returning to Des Moines, a place I knew and felt safe in.

I was convinced to leave by an incident one night while parked in what I later learned was not a great neighborhood. I was sound asleep in my bus on a cold August night when I was awakened by a crash and the whole bus shaking. I thought a car had hit me. As I sat up, I noticed the shadow of an arm reaching in through the front wing window. I yelled, "Hey!" as loud as I could, mostly out of fear. Thankfully, they ran off. They had thrown a brick through the window. Had I not been there, they would have gotten my guitar, amp, clothes, and the remaining $234 I had stashed under my bed.

I got up front, started the bus, and drove to the nearest gas station. I cleaned out as much glass as I could, then parked in front of the police station for the rest of the night. The next day, I gathered up Lumpy's drums and got the hell out of San Francisco. Things did not work out for me there.

It was an adventure, to say the least, but not what I had hoped. There was no effort on the part of Charles and Tim to include me in anything. The band fantasy never came about. I met no one, barely saw Charles and Tim, and spent most of my time wandering. I had no plan for when I got back to Des Moines, but for some reason, I was looking forward to returning to familiar places.

I left by myself. Escaped, as it were. I planned my route home. This was 1988, a time without cell phones and GPS, so I was using my trusty Road Atlas that I had borrowed from my parents. I decided to take U.S. Highway 50 outside of Sacramento. Having just read *Blue Highways* by William Least Heat-Moon, it looked like the perfect road less traveled.

U.S. 50 runs east and west, 3,000 miles across the middle of the country, from West Sacramento to Ocean City, Maryland. It is a mostly rural highway with small towns that pop up along the way. In Nevada and western Utah, there are incredible views of vast open land, mountains, rock formations, blue skies, sand, and a whole lot of nothingness. The section of U.S. 50 that runs through Nevada is called the "Loneliest Road in America." There are signs that say this on the highway. This was astonishing to me. It felt like I had discovered a lost highway, a road that was mystical and magical. Turns out U.S. 50 was an ancient Native American path over 200 years ago, and it felt sacred.

There was an incredible sense of being alone with your thoughts for so long that it could be unnerving for some. Fortunately, I have—and had—lived in my own head, isolated for most of my life, so it was no problem. It was like driving in space at times. There were no reference points to ground you: no people, cars, buildings, life of any kind to bounce your existence off of. You could see forever, and I rarely saw another car. Ironically, the only other vehicle I did see was another VW bus going the opposite way. We gave the "brotherhood and sisterhood of the bus" hello as we passed, and I learned something very important from that brief encounter: they were riding with their engine hood up to allow more airflow for cooling the engine. Why didn't I think of that! I was very concerned about my bus overheating in the Nevada desert, in the middle of nowhere, breaking down with no chance of help. I pulled over, lifted my back hood, and took off again.

There were times when I worried about finding gas in this vast nothingness. The desert is a dangerous place, and I was not prepared for breaking down. I had no water and very little food. I finally made it to Ely, Nevada just before running out of gas. As I drove on, it began to get dark and rain. It poured and poured.

This next part of my journey became a bit confusing, because I'm not sure what happened. It's possible I took a wrong turn, or that the road just seemed to change drastically, or that I was getting extremely road-weary. The highway turned into back roads, almost dirt roads at times. I was not sure I was still on Highway 50—but this much I do know:

There began to be mass numbers of frogs on the road. I mean thousands, and thousands of them. At first, I wasn't sure what they were. Mind you, it was pouring down rain, dark, and I was on an unfamiliar road. At first, I tried to slow down and swerve to miss them, but it was futile. They were everywhere. There was no missing them. They were indeed frogs, blanketing the road, jumping and squishing and crunching under my wheels. I flinched, convulsed and sometimes screamed with every frog I killed. The sound was revolting and turned my stomach. I couldn't pull off the road because there seemed to be no shoulder that I could see. Yet the road was abandoned, and there were no other cars.

Finally, the carnage ended, and the frogs were no longer on the road before me. I pushed on and finally reached an intersection where I could see signs to an interstate. I made it back to Des Moines two days later, found a nice quiet street, and slept until I was awakened by people going to work and the sound of everyday life.

I loved this time in my life. I lived in my bus, travelled all over the country, wrote songs and performed them at various coffee shops and cafes, and above all else felt free, truly free. I had no girlfriend to mess up my mind and to complicate things. I had very few possessions and no job. I really cannot remember where I got the money to live. I grew my hair out and lived the life of a vagabond hippie. Ah, but life has a way of finding you even when you're hiding in a 1970 VW Bus on the streets of Des Moines, Iowa. The carefree happy hippy life on the streets was about to end.

Sex and Love and Marriage

"He mistakes her love for sex; she mistakes his sex for love."
-From the song "Sex and Love"
-me

You only get married for the first time once, or so they say. When I first met Andra in 1987, I was living in an apartment in a huge Tudor-style mansion across the street from the Des Moines Art Center and Greenwood Park. It was known as "The Butler House" and had been built in 1923. It was a unique building with ornate craftsmanship both outside and in. The mansion had been divided into several apartments.

Andra originally moved into the mansion with her boyfriend, in the apartment across the hall from me. We had little interaction, if any, during that time. When she and her live-in boyfriend broke up, she moved into the apartment directly above me, and we started seeing each other more frequently in passing.

At the time, I was involved with Moon, but I could tell Andra was very interested in me. She was, quite frankly, one gorgeous woman. I was definitely attracted to her—what red-blooded American guy wouldn't be? I began to see her more often at gigs and parties, and every time I did, she made it clear she was into me. When Moon wasn't around, she was even more forward.

As my relationship with Moon became strained, I could feel my will to resist Andra slipping. I mean, what the hell is a twenty-something guy supposed to do when a gorgeous woman makes it clear she wants you? When I got back from San Francisco, we started hanging out more and more. I held her off as long as I could, until I had completely ended things with Moon.

It turned into a very sexual relationship, right from the start. As I got to know her better, Andra told me she had been sexually abused as a child by her grandfather. Because of that abuse, she had developed a serious infection that required drastic surgery, leaving her unable to have children. That hit me hard. I felt horrible for her…. angry, too—and an immense sense of compassion.

I had just quit my job, moved out of my swanky apartment, and gotten the VW bus, so once again it was time for an adventure. Andra and I decided to take a road trip to New Orleans and then over to my parents' place in North Carolina. It was supposed to be a fun trip with a beautiful woman, but it turned into something more than that.

We had fun…. lots of it. From the very beginning, she was all over me, and I didn't put up any defense. Hell, we pulled off I-35 South just a few miles outside Des Moines and had sex in the bus, with semi-trucks roaring by just feet away.

We drove south through Texas, taking some back roads along the way.

At one point, we stopped at a roadside fruit and vegetable stand. When we went up to pay, the old man looked at us and said, "You kids aren't from around here, are you? You best be careful and stick to the main highways." That was a strange, unsettling thing to hear. two hippy-looking kids in a flower-painted VW bus in the middle of bum-fuck Texas. We took his advice and got back on the main roads.

We headed down to Padre Island and camped on the beach for a couple of days, then drove east toward New Orleans. We found a campsite about twenty minutes outside the city and cleaned up before heading in.

When Andra got dressed, I felt uneasy. She came out in a short mini skirt, high boots, and a low-cut top. She looked incredibly hot, no denying that—but I could already see the kind of attention she was going to get. I told her straight up that I didn't want to spend the night dealing with guys trying to mess with us. Maybe I was a little insensitive, but it felt excessive, hell, even dangerous—walking into a city like New Orleans dressed like that.

She got a little embarrassed, and I felt bad about it, but she changed into jeans. We headed into the city and spent a few days exploring the French Quarter. After that, we hit the road again toward my parents' place in North Carolina.

That trip ended up being another major fork in the road for both of us.

From the beginning, Andra did not get along with my mother, but my father, who was manic at the time, was quite taken with her. They got along very well. We stayed for a couple of days, went down to the beach as often as we could, and then took off for the return trip to Des Moines.

While we were at my parents' house, I had told them privately that Andra was just a friend, nothing serious. Unfortunately, Andra saw our relationship very differently.

The drive back to Des Moines was interesting, to say the least. Somewhere in the Blue Ridge Mountains, the accelerator cable on the bus snapped. A 1970 VW Bus is kind of like a lawn mower in some ways. The accelerator cable hooks to the pedal, then runs all the way back to the engine, where it connects to a lever that opens and closes the throttle. The cable itself costs about three dollars to replace and is fairly easy to install, but there was no way to find an automotive store on Labor Day weekend in the middle of nowhere in the mountains of North Carolina.

I coasted off the road and pulled into a parking area with no clue what to do. Then, just by chance, I looked down and spotted a spring on the ground. (Random huh?) I attached the spring where the accelerator cable had connected to the engine and basically rigged it so the throttle stayed wide open all the time. There was no way to control our speed except by depressing the clutch and putting the bus in neutral.

When I started the engine, it immediately kicked into full acceleration mode. I put it in second gear, eased out the clutch as gradually as I could, and we took off. Once we got on the highway, we did pretty well climbing the mountains, but coming down was a little hairy. We would start going too fast with the throttle stuck wide open, so I'd shut off the engine, put the bus in neutral, and ride the momentum to the bottom. Then I'd turn the engine back on, pop the clutch in third gear, and off we'd go up the next mountain.

It worked pretty well until it started to rain. The electrical system in my bus was a little messed up, so when I turned off the engine, the wipers and headlights went off too. That made things dangerous fast, so we pulled off the road and slept for the night at the nearest campsite.

The next day there was no rain, so we pushed on. It was pretty amusing stopping for gas. I had to be really careful with the clutch and acceleration pulling up to the pump. You can imagine the looks we got as the bus came roaring and jerking in at full throttle until I killed the engine. Then I'd start it back up in full acceleration mode, work the clutch in and out, and somehow lurch us back onto the highway.

We made it back to Des Moines, but not before one final stop, when I tried to tell Andra I was ending the relationship. I wanted to tell her that I didn't love her, that she was a good friend, and that we had had a lot of fun, but I did not want it to become something serious. I just did not love her.

I told her that last night before we reached Des Moines, in the small but somehow infinite space inside a 1970 VW Bus. It did not go well. It was a very dark night. She was deeply hurt and upset. I felt terrible, but I was trying to be honest. A person should not stay in a relationship just because they don't want to hurt someone. That was the mistake I was trying not to make.

As we later found out, Andra was pregnant.

This trip was another great fork in the road for both of us. It had far-reaching consequences in both our lives and in my daughter's. Fate? Bad judgment? Free will? Am I just a pawn in some ambiguous, random world where there are only choices and consequences? What would have happened if I had chosen differently? Yet another fork in the road. It's like the damn Price Is Right. Door number one, two, or three?

I was compelled to do the right thing even though it was not the right thing in my heart. We were married at the Little Brown Church in the Veil in some small town in Iowa. I got my job back at the insurance company, we bought a house together and I tried for two years to make it work, but it was not in me. Out of this came the most beautiful little girl in the world, my daughter Lauren, who was conceived in a 1970 VW Bus somewhere between Des Moines, New Orleans, and Wilmington, North Carolina.

Intermission #1

"No amount of anxiety makes any difference to anything that is going to happen."

-Alan Watts

I am having good days and bad days. Today is a little rough. I've decided to stop taking my antidepressants because they aren't helping. I probably didn't give them enough time, but they seemed to be making me feel worse. You're not supposed to stop cold turkey, but I'm doing it anyway. I'm tired of all the medicine.

The anxiety is there now, but I've been able to sleep somewhat. I take a Lorazepam to get through parts of the day. The days and nights pass, and I try not to get overwhelmed by the infinite possibilities, but it's a fragile existence.

I miss doing something important. Some days I regret retiring from teaching. If I could have seen the madness as normal—just part of life, "those crazy kids being kids"—maybe it would have been different. But I couldn't do it. Couldn't fake it. Couldn't stand there and watch it all fall apart.

Trauma. Trauma. Too much trauma.

The Great Flood

"Blizzards, floods, volcanos, hurricanes, earthquakes: They fascinate because they nakedly reveal that Mother Nature, afflicted with bipolar disorder, is as likely to snuff us as she is to succor us."

-Dean Koontz

The floods of 1993 were epic. In fact, they're known as the "Great Flood of 1993," one of the most costly and devastating floods in U.S. history. The Mississippi and Missouri Rivers were the main culprits, swelling into tributaries and smaller rivers across the Midwest, including the two that run through Des Moines, the Raccoon River and the Des Moines River.

Much of the city became inaccessible. The water treatment plant was overtaken, and raw sewage poured into the Des Moines River. About 250,000 residents were without water for over two weeks; no showers, no toilets, no washing clothes or dishes, no drinking water. Drinking stations were set up, supplied from outside sources, including canned water from Anheuser-Busch. Roads and businesses shut down. Around 40,000 residents were also without electricity.

It was during this time that my divorce from Andra was being finalized. She and my daughter Rain were visiting my parents in North Carolina when the floods hit and ended up staying an extra week because of the conditions back home.

The divorce was uncontested, but I gave up a lot, as in the house we had bought together with help from my parents, and a new car financed through a loan from my sister. I wanted my daughter to live in a decent place, and I wanted out. So, I agreed.

Meanwhile, I was living in my VW bus on the streets of Des Moines.

Strangely, the summer of 1993 was one of the happiest times of my life. I was divorced, free from a dishonest relationship, and living on my own terms. I had grown my hair out, was writing songs, and performing solo at coffee shops and small venues around the city. I had one key to my name, the key to my bus and that was enough.

I would drive around, find a quiet street to park on, and spend my time reading, playing guitar, and sleeping. I'd play a few sets at local coffee shops, collect a few bucks, and hang out with friends. In the mornings, I'd head to a park, fire up my little stove, and make tea.

There were downsides. Living in a bus means dealing with things most people don't think about, like having to pee in the middle of the night. Sometimes I'd lean out the window. Eventually, I kept a gallon jug handy.

The worst part, though, was the mosquito trucks. The floods had turned the city into a breeding ground for mosquitos, and every night those trucks would roll through, spraying chemical fog. I'd hear the apocalyptic buzz of the fogger coming and scramble to close the windows before the fumes filled the bus. It was brutally hot that summer. Sometimes I'd go to the grocery store just to stand in the frozen food aisle, opening and closing the freezer doors for relief.

I didn't sleep much, but it didn't seem to matter.

I was the man around town. Free and easy.

This free and easy ended when the cold weather came. I lasted until October, but it got too cold and I had to rent an inexpensive piece of shit one room apartment above the Theatrical Shop in West Des Moines. It was nasty with shag orange carpet and one shared bathroom down the hall that was usually quite disgusting. Clogged toilet, clogged shower drain. My room had one window that looked out over the cold dark parking lot of old West Des Moines. The bed sagged horrifically in the middle. I often pissed in the sink because it was cleaner. It was all I could afford at the time. Eventually I got to a nicer place and was able to have my daughter over for visits.

Things have a way of working out exactly how they were meant to. Ha! After my divorce, I had a few girlfriends, some more serious than others. I played a lot of tennis, recorded some of my own music, traveled again to New Orleans in the bus with a girl I loved very much, and eventually bought a small house with help from my mother. Saved again!

In 1995 my father passed away. He died in his sleep. We held a small service for him in Wilmington, North Carolina, and, at his request, had him cremated. When we picked up the box of ashes, the funeral director asked what we planned to do with them. We told him we were going to scatter them in the ocean, just as my father had wanted. He replied that doing so was illegal unless we went seven miles out to sea. We told him we would, knowing full well we would not. My father would have loved that.

We took the box of still-warm ashes out to dinner with us, along with a couple bottles of champagne, to a restaurant overlooking the ocean. Afterward, we walked to the end of the pier to scatter him. We took turns grabbing warm handfuls of ashes and throwing them into the air. Sometimes they blew back into our faces and hair. We cried, and we said things that made us laugh, and then we went home to my mother's house.

It was surreal, to say the least. That was it, seventy-five years of living, and it was over. I hope he had a good life. He definitely had his fair share of suffering. My father used to say that his goal in life was not to be happy but rather to reach some kind of contentment. I hope that he did so. If the way we die is any indication of how we lived, then he definitely lived well. I wonder what he would say about his life? I feel as if I barely knew him.

My dear, sweet mother found a renewed life after grieving for my father for about a year. She had had a rough life with him at times, being the wife of a minister, living through his deep depressions and overwhelming manic swings. I suspect she felt some of that burden lift when he passed.

She made a wonderful new friend, Louise, and they had a blast together. They traveled to Scotland and England and were inseparable for several years. My mother created a beautiful garden in her backyard and stayed active.

Then, out of nowhere, Louise cut her off. No explanation. Just gone. My mother never understood it, and it haunted her.

From that point on, her health began to decline. She fell and injured herself. She developed severe, debilitating anxiety that left her a mess; something I didn't understand at the time, but do now. Eventually, she moved into a retirement home near my oldest sister in Doylestown, where she received some assistance.

I spoke with her as often as I could and visited a couple of times with my family. Within a few years, she developed colon cancer and died in hospice care just weeks after the diagnosis.

My last conversation with her was the day before she died. It was light, even funny, nothing that would have made me think she had only hours left. She sounded happy. Alert.

I spoke at her memorial service and broke down several times.

I have regrets.

I wish I had told her how much I loved her, how much she meant to me. I wish I had told her that I understood her anxiety. That I could have been more patient, more compassionate. I wish I had comforted her more, the way she had comforted me so many times.

I remember when she got into a car accident near my school. I was embarrassed instead of concerned. I should have stopped. I should have stayed with her.

I remember when she asked me to lie down with her because her anxiety was overwhelming. I didn't. I should have.

She used to joke, "What have I done to piss God off so much?" But it wasn't really a joke.

She was my light, and I don't think I ever told her that. Her intelligence, wit, charm, grace, and sarcasm were always there, even when I didn't see them.

It strikes me now as infinitely sad that we never really know our parents.... not fully. There's a line they don't cross, and a line we don't want them to cross. They protect us from parts of themselves, and we avoid seeing too much. I know this from being a parent myself.

We never truly know the hopes and dreams, the sadness and joy, the dissatisfaction and contentment of our parents. At best, we get brief, unguarded moments—when they drop the roles of parent—and for a second, allow us to see who they really are.

Intermission #2

"Don't assume I'm weak because I have panic attacks. You'll never know the amount of strength it takes to face the world every day."

-Unknown

Lately I've been having these daily fits of outright sobbing. Blubbering, crying, and hollering in anguish about what seems to be an overwhelming sadness beyond my control. I was listening to the Decemberists yesterday and blubbered after 20 minutes of listening. Today I watched a movie (The Fundamentals of Caring) that overwhelmed me with how random life is and how tragedy is beset upon some. This amazing ability of humans to overcome and keep going through terrible things just wrecks me sometimes. I am also sobbing about how grateful I am to not have gone through a tragedy. Even as I write and think that statement, I feel uncomfortable and afraid that I may have just jinxed my family. I do not believe that I am strong enough to survive a family tragedy. I am sobbing, it feels good, I am alive, yet I am afraid. I don't think this is normal. I have resisted too much medication to treat my depression and anxiety because I feel as if I can overcome, or deal with it. I don't want to cloud up my emotional experiences with chemicals that alter me. But I don't know how much longer I can go on like this. *Is there some sort of drug that will make me feel good? Do I really want to take that drug?* I weep and I suck it up. I write and it leaves me alone for a little while. Blessed relief!

Empathy for the Devil

"Be kind. For everyone you meet is fighting a battle you know nothing about."
-Ian Maclaren

Went to the dermatologist yesterday for my annual cancer scare. I had a few strange-looking spots checked out. A risky endeavor, for sure. I had spent days in intense anxiety before the visit, and the day of the appointment was especially bad, because I was pretty sure I had cancer.

As I stepped off the elevator on my way to the dermatologist, there was a woman in the lobby, sobbing into her phone. I overheard what she was saying. "It has spread to the lungs and into the lymph glands," she said through her tears. I wasn't sure whether she was talking about herself or a close relative. Either way, I instantly felt horrible for her. The pain and agony of just having learned something like that could be heard in her sobbing. This poor woman was facing a potential death sentence and was clearly devastated and hopeless.

I wanted to sit down beside her and try to comfort her somehow, but I realized that probably would not have been appropriate. And truthfully, I could not find the courage to do it. I began to feel pathetic and small for my own self-induced fears and troubles. My thoughts turned inward, and my anxiety and depression intensified. I could feel her anguish.

Anxiety, for me, is thinking too big. It is allowing the whole world's problems and suffering to find their way into my consciousness and consume me, along with our family's possible problems as well. What could go wrong, I asked myself? A lot of things, that's what. Must stop. Must put these thoughts out of mind. Must forget, or at least minimize, that woman's pain and suffering and push it out of my consciousness for my own sake.

That same day, there was another humbling moment at the dermatologist's office. While I was waiting in the examining room, I could hear a conversation in the room next door. It was a woman with her baby. The baby was having some kind of problem with his eyes, and there was talk of experimental drugs being used.

How ridiculous I felt. How petty it seemed to be consumed by my own anxiety and fear over nothing. I have been so lucky, so fortunate, even blessed, if you will. These tragedies are happening all around us. There are people sitting right next to us who are going through emotional hell and still trying to hold themselves together.

There are so many brave people in this world. Brave beyond belief. Brave not by choice, but by circumstance. I am not one of them. I feel like a coward, a pathetic, self-centered coward.

I got a call today from the dermatologist. Pre-cancerous something or other. "Call us if it comes back or gets scaly again." Very reassuring, thank you. Whew!

Things have not been going well the last few days. I was okay for a couple of weeks, and then it came back. Anxiety. A surge of it.

Physically, my RA is starting to concern me. I'm stiffer, more sore. My hands feel weaker. This is how it started before. My feet, ankles, and knees ache. It feels like I'm one step away from a wheelchair, from not being able to work.

That scares me. A lot.

Must keep going. Must push on.

I went back on Methotrexate, that evil yellow drug I inject into my leg. It makes me sick. I was off it for a few months, but the RA started creeping back. So, I chain myself to it again, trying to keep the joint monster away.

In the last couple of weeks, I've had two broken teeth, a frozen shoulder and a suspicious skin spot biopsied. And now the RA symptoms again.

"Nibbled to death by ducks," my dad used to say.

That's what it feels like. Not one big collapse. Just a slow breakdown.

I can't let myself think that way. That's how things get bad, fast.

Today I had looked up possible ways to kill myself using the drugs that I have around the house. Just in case. I forgot to delete my history on the computer and my wife discovered what I had been doing.

She insisted that I go to the hospital. She convinced me it would be the best thing to do. I capitulated reluctantly. Nothing really came out of it. They didn't have a room for me so I stayed in a small room in the intake part of the psych ward. They got me a cot, gave me some drugs and checked on me regularly. I lay awake the entire night. In the morning a nice woman came to talk to me about how I was feeling and then I went home the next day. I think it turned out to be a nice break for my wife not having to worry about me for a moment. But it didn't help me much and I did not seek the recommended additional care.

Sometimes I tell myself I'm not depressed—that I'm just bored. *It's not true.*

Everything feels flat. Nothing excites me. I think I need something new, something exciting, but I'm stuck inside responsibilities that leave me exhausted. I don't have the energy to break out. There's no joy.

There's an awareness that gets in the way of just living. I try to push past it.

Today I feel hopeless, even though it started well. I played tennis. Did a lot of yard work. *How is it possible that raking can cause me anxiety*? Then it rained.... something I used to love. But I just wanted to go to bed and stay there.

Time with my wife didn't help. I had the day off, but we couldn't decide what to do. Or maybe I couldn't. I went to bed anyway. Felt guilty, but couldn't do anything about it.

I stayed there until responsibility forced me back up.

I want to die.

I don't want to die.

She loves me.

She loves me not.

The Blues

"I never had the blues; the blues always had me."

-Brownie McGeee

You'd think being depressed and a musician, I'd like the blues. I don't. I hate them, the music, I mean. I've just never liked the blues. It's a bit like masturbation musically. Noodling about instrumentally and lyrically unimaginative.

I'm not an idiot. I know a lot of rock is rooted in the blues. Still, I find it boring, repetitive and uninspiring,

Lately I've had the urge to play guitar again. Nothing big; just to learn a song or two. That might do me some good.

It was my first love, after all.

Why did I sell my electric guitar?

Close Encounters of the Anxious Mind

"It is very hard to explain to people who have never known serious depression or anxiety the sheer continuous intensity of it. There is no off switch."

-Matt Haig

I had an encounter today with a woman at the desk of a fitness club where my son was playing tennis. She checked me in as a guest and asked about my son. As it turned out, her daughter is the same age, 13—and used to play tennis.

Then she told me her daughter had cancer. Liver and lungs. She'd had a liver transplant and was doing "okay." She asked about my son's program, thinking maybe she could get her daughter back into it.

"She loves tennis," she said. "We've just been very cautious. Maybe too cautious."

I told her about the program. We talked for a bit. It was a simple, easy conversation.

What struck me was her smile. She seemed steady. Positive. Even grateful.

And I stood there thinking about my own anxiety, my own depression, how much space it takes up. At any moment, something real could hit. Something that would demand actual courage.

She's already living in that.

People carry things you would never guess. They show up, smile, have conversations, and keep moving.

That takes something. That is strength. That is courage. Things I don't have.

For me, getting out of bed and making it through the day can feel like the challenge. It pales in comparison.

Nostalgia is a dangerous thing. The Oxford Dictionary defines nostalgia as "a sentimental longing or wistful affection for the past, typically for a period or place with happy personal associations." From Greek nostos 'return home' + algos 'pain'. I think the Greeks got it right again. Pain! Returning home to the memories of the past and feeling the pain knowing that that part of your life is over, never to return. A sense of great loss.

I like to call it the nostalgia effect. Painful sentimentality. Let's face it, you're going to lose your good looks, your youthful skin, your full head of hair, your nice teeth, the full use of your limbs, and suffer any number of maladies. Your affection for those past experiences and feelings of loss can be overwhelming. Nothing lasts! And I mean nothing. Everything changes. Thus, with old age and anxiety, nostalgia is a bit crippling for me to say the least.

My life seems to be filled with out of control nostalgia. The thoughts of this life concluding, and the pain of what life was like is crushing me. It is unbearable at times. The ability to accept my mortality and to enjoy my later years is something I have not been able to do. This is a skill that I must learn if I am to have a fighting chance to survive these days.

As you can probably tell I am constantly comparing myself to others and feeling inadequate. Everyone is better, richer, healthier, and happier than me. Dumb, I know, but can't help it. There is no real sense of safety in my existence. I get anxious about going out into the world, and I have panic attacks on what feels like a daily basis, often for no clear reason.

I can pull myself out of it for a while and distract myself with tasks, with my job, and with daily duties, but this is still my life. This is the life I have somehow created for myself. I see no real end to it, only the daunting task of trying to manage it for the sake of the ones I love. I hope I am up for it, but I am never fully convinced that I am.

There are brief moments when I lose that painful self-awareness, moments when the anxiety lifts and a few hours pass in relative calm. Those moments are good, and I am grateful for them. They remind me, however briefly, that another way of being is at least possible. I can only hope that someday the calm will begin to outweigh the anxiety, and that the future will not be filled with worry, fear, and tragedy.

Working as a grocery store cashier can be a little like being a bartender. People sometimes tell you things that are deeply personal and private.

As an observer, I notice things that are sometimes sad, sometimes absurd, and sometimes disturbing.

I see old friends and acquaintances come through my line. Yesterday I spoke with my old bass player, who seems to be struggling with depression. Do I know that for sure? No; but I can tell.

He told me about his best friend, who had just committed suicide. He had seen him only a few days earlier and thought everything was fine. His friend shot himself and left behind a teenage daughter.

Even though I didn't know the man, the story shook me. I felt my friend's pain, and the pain his friend must have been carrying. I know that edge more than I care to admit.

I see this old friend regularly, and we often struggle to talk to each other because we're both dealing with depression. It makes for a strangely lifeless conversation: two depressed middle-aged men trying to find something to talk about that isn't depressing.

Usually it goes nowhere. Just a look of acknowledgment, a small shake of the head, and an awkward silence heavy enough to kill.

There is a homeless girl who comes into the store every day and buys either a bag of frozen peas or frozen corn. She microwaves it and sits in the café with her headphones on, sometimes talking to herself while playing with tarot cards. Occasionally I've seen her using a laptop. She stays all day, sometimes until we close.

She can't be much older than twenty-two.

I want to talk to her. I want to know her story, and I want to help her. Yet I just watch and say nothing. I could offer her a place to stay in our home, but my wife and son might not like that. She could be dangerous, but I don't think so.

There are many lonely people who come through my checkout line, many of them elderly, who obviously look forward to the interaction. There are also many who suffer from illness and are searching for natural cures for their diseases.

Last night a camerawoman from the local television station came through my line. She was visibly upset. She told us about a horrific car accident she had just covered, and she began to cry right there in the checkout line. We all felt bad for her as she cried and said, "I can never forget some things…. they just stay with me."

It had never occurred to me the kinds of trauma news reporters must carry with them. She was still crying as she left the store.

I had been doing pretty well for the past few weeks. I hadn't experienced any severe anxiety or depression—just a few difficult days here and there. This week, however, has been rough.

I'm not sure why. There may be no reason at all, other than that my mind has been conditioned to feel anxiety and depression and does so whenever it wants.

Perhaps it was my son and wife being very sick multiple times over the past month. Illness represents a loss of my perceived control, and I struggle deeply with that loss. My hyperactive mind jumps to the worst possibilities, that my son or my wife have come down with some serious disease and could die from their sickness.

Worry feeds anxiety.

Selfishly I think of my own health when my family is sick. I have virtually no immune system because of the drugs I take for rheumatoid arthritis, so I'm afraid that I might end up in the hospital as well, or worse.

I should learn to be grateful for all that I have. I have a family that loves me. We are comfortable. I have a full-time job now that, along with my pension, meets our financial needs.

But I worry about money. It is a constant source of worry and anxiety. We live beyond our means, and I overcompensate by trying not to spend money at all, which only adds to my anxiety. Every expenditure feels like a dagger.

My work hours are not great for our family. But we march on…. hour by hour, day by day, week by week. Until what? What is the end goal, death? Retirement? The end of anxiety? Will that only come with death?

I take my son to school and then go back to bed. I feel guilty about this, but it beats the anxiety. I don't usually go back to sleep. Instead, I kill a couple of hours before the anxiety kicks in. Then I get ready for work.

I'm feeling low today. That's really the problem. I tell myself, "Today is a bad day," and I push through.

I need to remember that I have gotten better—much better. Sometimes I pick up my guitar and play a little, and I play tennis with a friend every week.

My wife should probably leave me.

I must get up now, get ready for work, put on a happy face, and fake it. Maybe I'll even play the guitar.

I am grateful for this moment. I am grateful for my wife and my son. I am grateful that I have a job.

Help me to be grateful; and let it be enough.

The Passing of Time

"Time is the wisest counselor of all."
-Pericles

I have been working as a full-time supervisor at the grocery store for almost two years now. The money has been decent, and the work is tolerable, sometimes even fun. I have made some new casual friends at the store and feel secure in my job.

I'm not sure how or when it happened but I no longer have crippling anxiety or depression. I guess it happened gradually with me not noticing. Remarkably I take no medication nor do I see a therapist.

It seems as though time and distance from the traumatic past of teaching have given me some peace. The routine of work and the return of the art of distraction have helped me heal.

I have stopped hyper-thinking about the future and hyper-worrying about it, settling instead into a kind of acceptance. I've found a niche that makes me believe things just might be okay. I think we will survive.

I remain cautious, reluctant to feel completely safe, knowing that severe anxiety and depression can return at any moment. But for now, I am okay. We are okay.

I'm playing lots of competitive tennis, exercising regularly, traveling on vacations with my family, and even living in the moment, something I once thought would never be possible again.

I am still a pessimist at heart and sarcastic as hell. I am definitely not happy or in any way satisfied, but maybe—just maybe…for me, that's okay. Life does not have to be grand or spectacular. Maybe life can simply be what it is. Maybe I can accept that life is random and ambiguous and just move on.

Maybe…

In the end, it is simply too hard to care too damn much about this sinking ship. It's going down one way or another, and you're going down with it; that much is certain. It's all about how you want to go. Do you go out with a whimper or a bang? Do you spend your time worrying about the ship going down, or do you distract yourself from the fact that it is?

I've chosen the latter.

Faking it takes a toll, though. Knowing the futility and hopelessness of it all and still carrying on is one of the most difficult things for me to do. Reconciling the suffering, cruelty, pain, and tragedy of the world with one's own life is not easy.

Even the beauty and goodness of this world feel bittersweet to me.

The world is dying. You're dying. Everyone is dying. And yet you still find a way to keep living, keep loving, keep trying, finding some small sliver of comfort and safety.

Living is the ultimate leap of faith. You just have to believe everything is going to be alright.

It's a belief I once lost and never expected to find again.

Everything will be whatever it wants to be. Que Sera, Sera (Whatever Will Be, Will Be); a song introduced, ironically, in Alfred Hitchcock's film *The Man Who Knew Too Much.*

So, get ready for the ride that keeps on giving and taking, and make it up as you go along.

Advance, recover. Advance, recover. Until the battle is over.

It makes no difference how much you worry. The result will simply be what it will be.

After its all said and done, it's just random and ambiguous anyway.

The End

"And in the end, the love you take, is equal to the love, you make"
-Lennon and McCartney

It came back.

It went away for five years, and then it returned. I thought I was free and clear. I got too comfortable, too complacent.

It came back harder, and with a vengeance. And this time there were no circumstances to blame—no middle school students, no post-traumatic stress. Just crippling anxiety and depression.

It had been lurking beneath the surface of what I had come to see as normal life: the day-to-day acceptance, the inherited gene pool, the underlying chaos, and the undeniable swings of manic energy.

I had made it through severe anxiety, depression, hopelessness, COVID, joblessness, and uncertainty. I had settled into a full-time supervisor job at the grocery store, then eventually gone part-time, embracing semi-retirement with a kind of relief.

We bought a camper and fixed it up, then went on several camping trips together. I bought a scooter and rode it around town with a smile on my face. I played tennis competitively, won every tournament I entered, and qualified for nationals. I swam twice a week. I bought a convertible Corvette and worked on it myself, spending far too much money on repairs. I drank too much. I went shopping for clothes, something I had rarely done before.

Friends who had known me for years said, I seemed different, jokingly accusing me of being happy. I was, in many ways, unrecognizable to them.

Looking back, I was not simply happy. I was something else; energized, expansive, and disconnected from the limits I normally lived within. But at the time, it felt like clarity. It felt like confidence. It felt like certainty.

Mania

If I'm being honest, being manic feels incredible. You feel invincible, and completely sure of yourself. Every day is exhilarating. There is a rush to it, an intensity that makes ordinary life feel distant and muted. Boring even.

I can only think of the things that led up to my inevitable crash, each one relatively small, but nevertheless.

It began with an injury to my foot that kept me from competing fully at the national tennis tournament. I played, but I couldn't play up to my potential. I was pretty down about this, but I seemed to accept it and move on.

However, I wasn't able to play tennis during the summer due to the foot injury and then a shoulder injury.

Next, I had fairly deep skin surgery to remove a suspicious mole on my back. It eventually got infected and took quite a long time to heal. This caused me to worry incessantly.

Our garage door broke. Our washing machine broke. We had mice in the house. It was piling up.

I decided to sell the Corvette I had wasted so much money on. I sold it to a buyer from New Jersey. That out-of-state transaction made me extremely nervous.

Blizzards and bitter cold. The impossible and endless task of shoveling out from underneath the continuous fall of snow. My son and wife getting sick. The constant worry about money. Lack of sleep. Changes at work that made it extremely hard to go in. And the looming question: *How are we going to afford to send our son to college?*

For most people, all of these things are just part of life, right?

But for me, it amounted to a severe loss of control, a loss of feeling safe, and a growing fear again about whether we were going to be okay. I lost the faith. We were not going to be okay. Fear. Fear and more fear. It doesn't make sense. It's irrational.

This can't be happening again.

My fear grew exponentially. Every day, paralyzing fear. Fear of nothing and everything. Fear of the unknown.

The switch was back on. The brain chemicals went haywire.

The gene pool ignited.

This was worse than my first bout.

Going to work began to become increasingly anxiety-provoking. Any event or function provoked anxiety. Anxiety led to depression. It took everything I had to make it through the day. Most days the anxiety was so draining that I would just lie on the couch agonizing, dreading, hiding my anxiety and depression from my son, from my wife. I couldn't function, I didn't want to go out. I sought isolation.

I began to think of ways to commit suicide that would look like accidents. I even rehearsed some of these thoughts. Sometimes I would let the car run in the garage with the door down for a little while.

I feel as though I am existing, not living. There is no joy for me in anything. I can't wait to go to bed. I want the day to be over. I'm finding it increasingly difficult to sleep. I take a pill.

Sometimes it works, sometimes it doesn't. Like tonight.

I am close to it. I am truly beside myself. I could really do it.

I can feel myself fading. Fading away in importance, fading away in relevance, becoming a memory of myself.

I have been a waste. A self-indulgent waste of time. I thought I was different than everyone else, but I'm not. I'm just a self-centered, egotistical narcissist. I am just trying to make it to the finish line.

Tomorrow is another day.

Can't wait to go to bed.

I'm holding dozens of pills in my hand, raising my hand to my mouth, pausing, shaking, almost. Maybe taking pills and getting in the tub, perhaps an accidental slip and fall and drowning. Must find a way out, but it must look like an accident. I'm either riddled with anxiety or lying in bed. I've lost twenty-five pounds. Can't eat. Unable to function. I went to see a couple of psychiatrists, but neither were helpful. Made things worse.

They offered me drugs which I took for maybe a week but felt that they weren't helping. (These drugs take several weeks to have any effect.) I tried to find a therapist but either couldn't get up the energy for the search or didn't like the ones that I met.

I have known this fear from before. This feels different, more severe, unrelenting. Fear is breaking me. I'm in a swirling spiral with no way out. Nothing helps, every day is torture, I can only think of one way out. This morning I decided. I can't bear it anymore, I need it to end, I want it to end. It is the only option.

I'm going to kill myself.

How many people attempt suicide in the United States? According to the CDC in 2022, 13.2 million people had seriously thought about suicide, 3.8 planned for suicide and 1.6 attempted suicide. That's millions. Failed attempted suicides generally run about 25 per every suicide attempt. Suicide is the 11th leading cause of death in the United States and there were about 49,000 people who died by suicide in 2022. White males account for 68% of all suicide deaths in the U.S. and firearms accounted for about 55% of all suicide deaths.

I guess it was a good thing that our family did not own a firearm, because on that Tuesday morning in April, just days past my sixty-fourth birthday I had decided. I had had enough fear, enough suffering and enough hopelessness that I just couldn't go on anymore. I called in sick for work. I gathered a large assortment of drugs, Trazadone, Xanax, Ativan, and pain killers. I'm not sure how many. I swallowed them in handfuls. I put on a mask thinking that it would help me suffocate. I went to bed at 8:00 am in the morning hoping it would be my last day. My wife was at work, and my son was at school. I didn't think about anything but to put an end to my suffering. I didn't think about who would find me, I didn't think about the pain and suffering I would cause to my family. I didn't think about my son and daughter and the legacy I would leave to them. This was the only way. I was at the lowest point of desperation. I just couldn't take the fear anymore.

I swallowed all of them.

I don't remember much after taking the pills. People were yelling, asking me questions, picking me up and doing things to me that I didn't understand. I woke up in the hospital very hazy and in a cloud with a stranger sitting in a chair across the room. I was disappointed that I had not been successful. To be honest, I don't remember much about the hospital stay. The only thing that sticks out to me is the attending physician telling me that I "had" to go into a psyche ward inpatient facility. There were no ifs ands or buts. I had to, it was the law or the hospital policy. Anyone who attempts to take their own life must not be dismissed from the hospital without first doing some time in the psych ward. I had no choice.

The hospital that I was staying in had an inpatient mental health facility, so three days after my initial hospital stay, I was taken in the middle of the night with a security escort to be admitted to this mental health ward. My wife was not allowed to go past the doors leading into the ward. I was searched, I was asked questions by two nurses in a secluded room, my things were inventoried, I was given a pair of light blue scrubs and some socks. I was then taken to another room by one of the nurses to be examined. She took my temperature.

She took my blood pressure but while she was doing so the pressure on my arm became unbearable. "This doesn't seem normal" I said. "It's really painful." She took it off my arm and said something like "this must not be working." I should have known this as an omen. A bad omen. I was then taken to my room which I shared with another man who was snoring like a drunken sailor. The door was closed, left slightly ajar and I lay awake all night long listening to snoring and heavy magnetic doors opening and closing. A nurse would enter the room every hour or so to look in on us. It looked like they were checking to see if my roommate was still breathing. The dank smell of old urine from the sheets and the constant awareness that someone was watching me on the video camera in the room made it impossible to sleep. My thoughts of desperation began to take hold.

The bathroom was simple: no shower curtain, no toilet seat, no towels, just one soap dispenser and a stack of paper towels. Evidently, a toilet seat could be used as a weapon, and a shower curtain as a noose. I was confused and afraid. This was not good. It did not feel safe. It did not seem like a place where I was supposed to get better.

Someone came into the room and wrote something on the chalkboard. It was some sort of daily goal, along with the names of our nurse and nurse's assistant. I remember looking at it and thinking: how can I convince my keepers that I've reached that goal? The goal on the board was never changed. I don't remember what it was.

In the morning, I heard people talking and a television blaring religious programming. I didn't know what I was supposed to do; whether I was meant to stay in my room or go out. There was no clock in the room. What time was it?

The night before had been a blur. I couldn't remember anything about the setup of the facility, and I had no information about where or when I was supposed to leave my room.

A nurse came in and pricked my roommate's finger for a diabetic check. After she left, I wandered into the hallway and saw a few people sitting in a large common room. It had several tables and chairs, a plastic couch, and a couple of plastic love seats. Everything felt hard, cold, and synthetic.

A nurse's assistant approached me and took my temperature and blood pressure. I would later learn this was a routine procedure, done every morning and again before bed. There was also a medication distribution time. Everyone received their medications in the morning and at night. I'm not sure what I was given at the time.

A cart was wheeled down the long hallway at the far end of the facility; the female wing, I would later learn. It was breakfast.

I sat and watched as more and more patients emerged from their rooms, all dressed in standard pale blue scrubs and socks. They lined up for breakfast, and a nurse handed each person a tray. No one spoke. It was strange—no one spoke. They received their food and returned to their tables in complete silence.

I went last. I picked up my tray and sat down uneasily in an empty chair. There was nothing to say. I kept my head down, ate what I could, returned my tray, and went back to my room.

I made my bed and lay down. After a while, I got up again and returned to the common area. A few people were coloring at a table. Three or four were watching television. Two men paced the hallways.

One of them looked frightening; like a caged animal, endlessly circling his enclosure. He seemed on the verge of violence. The other paced in the opposite direction across the room, his tongue hanging out as if trying to catch raindrops from the air.

I sat in an open chair in front of the television and watched. I would occasionally return to my room, but my roommate slept most of the time except during meals and medication rounds.

Lunch came, then dinner, then the 8:00 p.m. snack and medication round, followed by bedtime.

There was a sense of hopelessness in this place that was palpable. A languid smell that I will never forget, and am sometimes reminded of. I began to think of this place as a prison. It was a place to house mostly drug and alcohol addicts, to stabilize them for a week or so, then release them until the next relapse.

Many of the patients, I learned, were regulars there. Others had been there for months. I was the only person who had attempted suicide. My roommate, Jim, had called the police saying he was going to kill himself, but he had not actually attempted it. He was schizophrenic, I later found out. He had false teeth and would take them out every night, placing them on the desk between our beds. In the morning, he would put them back in. He never cleaned or brushed them the entire time I was his roommate.

There was another man who had threatened to run into traffic, but beyond that, most of the patients were addicts. One woman had no teeth and cried and sobbed in her room so loudly that her cries echoed through the facility.

Another man seemed like a walking zombie, heavily sedated, coming out of his room only for meals and medication before returning to sleep. He had been there over four months. His name was John.

In fact, many patients existed this way. They emerged only for meals, then returned to their rooms to sleep until the next was served. My roommate was the same: sleep, eat, repeat.

Because I had been admitted to the psych ward on the weekend, there were no doctors and no group therapy sessions. I spent that long first weekend trying to learn the routine and remain inconspicuous, so as not to stand out from the others.

Most nights were sleepless. The opening and closing of heavy magnetic doors made too much noise for me to ignore. I had always been a light sleeper, but the constant clanging made rest nearly impossible. I lay awake, aware of the camera watching me, tossing and turning. Both shoulders ached to the point that I could only find comfort on my back.

I must have injured my left shoulder when I fell out of bed; I remember being stuck between the bed and the nightstand when I was first found. I remember people asking if I could get up, and me trying so hard, but being unable to free myself.

Lying there awake, I began to worry and obsess over the cost of this incarceration. We were going to be broke, I thought. Would insurance even cover an attempted suicide? How much would this all cost…thousands, tens of thousands, maybe even hundreds of thousands?

Every morning was the same. The nurse's assistants; who seemed to be either in their late seventies or barely out of high school, would take my blood pressure and temperature. Then the nurses would come around to distribute medications and ask the same questions every day.

From that first weekend, I had one goal: to get out of there. Not to get better or recover, but to leave as soon as possible. I always answered the nurses' questions in a way that I thought would help that goal. No, I would not hurt myself. No, I did not have suicidal thoughts. Yes, my anxiety and depression were about a 5 out of 10. No, I did not feel hopeless. And no, I did not feel safe.

There were many things about the place that I would come to see as unbearable, but one immediate physical issue was the cold. It was freezing, and the floors were bitterly cold. My feet were constantly numb and in pain, and I found myself always trying to warm them.

It wasn't until Monday of that first week that a doctor came to see me. He was a Pakistani man with a noticeable limp. We met in a room that I came to think of as both the sentencing room and the parole room. It was visible from the hallway, patients could walk by and see inside. It felt like a room of both hope and despair. Everyone knew that being called in meant a decision: discharge or continued stay. When patients left, you could usually tell which outcome they'd received.

Each patient waited for the moment they might be called in when the doctor arrived on the ward.

I asked him about his foot, assuming it was an injury, thinking it might be a way to connect. He said it was a birth defect. We both felt awkward from the start. Things were not off to a great beginning.

He asked me the same questions I would hear repeatedly during my stay; from nurses, doctors, anyone doing an assessment. He prescribed me two medications for depression, one for sleep at night, which was an antipsychotic, and a medication to take as needed for anxiety.

I thought I might be there for a week at most. Unfortunately, that would not be the case. To this day, I couldn't tell you exactly how long I was in that hell.

Every day felt like an eternity of worry, fear, anxiety, intense self-awareness, and survival. Every night was spent sleepless, thinking about the financial and emotional burden I had put on my family, listening to the heavy doors opening and closing and the deep, unsettling snores from my roommate.

I began to receive calls from my wife and family members. There were two portable phones for patients to use, but there was no privacy; taking them into your room was not allowed. Nurses often seemed annoyed by the calls I received. I would walk up and down the hallways with the phone, under the scrutiny of patients and staff. At times, I felt the stares of both unsettling. I felt uncomfortable receiving calls and, at times, burdened by them. I wanted to be left alone. I wanted to get out.

I received calls almost every day, sometimes multiple times a day, while other patients rarely received any. My sisters, daughter, and wife called several times a week. I was grateful for the contact, but it felt strained talking to them after having attempted suicide. How do you converse after something like that? I was ashamed.

I was especially ashamed for my son. I didn't want him to visit me and see me in that place. I called him once or twice to tell him I was sorry and that I loved him, but the shame was too much to bear.

As it turned out the doctor with the limp was the on-call doctor for the day. The main doctor of this facility was named Dr. Richard. He was a self-righteous man who seemed to enjoy his power. He spoke arrogantly and with no compassion. I disliked him from the first time we met. He was the quintessential evil warden of the prison just like I had seen in movies.

My first meeting with him did not go well. I wanted to get out, and I told him that this hospital was not set up to help me and that this was going to ruin my family financially. He said, "if you want out you need to come up with a plan." I was a little freaked out at this point and probably came across as very unstable. (Which I was.) But he was no help. This was a doctor who was clearly in it only for the ride. How was I to come up with a plan? I was in no condition to come up with a plan. I thought he was the doctor, where was his plan for me? He was one smug son of a bitch. I left that meeting feeling awful, pissed off and hopeless. I asked for the phone after that meeting and called my wife. I told her that this place was awful and I needed to get out. I put her in a terrible place. She was angry and afraid and with good reason wanted me to get better before I came home. She needed me to be in a safe place where I wouldn't hurt myself yet I begged to get me out. I was desperate.

Every day, we had to choose from a menu what we wanted for breakfast, lunch, and dinner for the following days. This became an unexpected source of anxiety. Something as simple as picking food from a menu should have been easy, but it wasn't. I agonized over my choices every time.

As I said before, every day felt like an eternity. I paced up and down the hallway, watched TV, spoke with family members who called, and fought off anxiety. I was determined not to ask the nurses for anxiety medication, even though I felt terrible. Sometimes I would just lie in my room.

Asking nurses for anything was not received well. One nurse in particular seemed annoyed by any request and frequently discouraged patients from taking anxiety medication, claiming it wasn't helping them. She seemed void of compassion.

Some afternoons there were "therapy" meetings in the main area. I use that word loosely, as they were not especially helpful and were mainly directed toward an audience of addicts. They were usually run by a hard-nosed, no-nonsense former addict who would not tolerate non-participation or distractions from patients milling about. I did not enjoy these sessions, nor did I get much from them. I attended because they helped pass the time, and because I thought it made me look like a better candidate for getting out of there.

At no point did I receive individual therapy. Not once.

Sometimes there was art therapy, which mostly consisted of coloring. There was also music therapy, which involved a young woman playing songs on a guitar. It was awkward. Again, I attended mainly for appearance's sake.

When it was warm enough, we would go out into the courtyard and play basketball or walk around. It was there, during my most desperate times, that I began to plan my escape.

I was still suicidal; let's face it, this place felt like it was making things worse. I planned on climbing the fence and running to the bridge two blocks away. That bridge stood at least fifty feet above the Des Moines River, and I knew there was a small, dangerous dam about 100 yards downstream. People had died going over it before.

I would jump from that bridge and drown, and that would be that. I thought about it every time we were outside.

My wife would come to visit me during allowed visitation times. Visitation offered no privacy as it was held in the main room where patients would congregate. Some other patients would have family visits at the same time. Other patients would pace back and forth during these visits. I often begged my wife to get me out. She was in contact with the evil doctor and had convinced him that I was bipolar. Reluctantly he prescribed medication for this diagnosis and my stay continued for weeks. Weeks and weeks of going through the same shit every day.

Sleepless nights, anxiety ridden days, drunks and addicts coming and going and me trying to convince my doctor and nurses that I was ready to go back into the real world. It didn't work. One day my roommate asked me what I was in for. He called me "guy." I told him I tried to kill myself. Curiously, he asked me specifically how and what drugs I had used. It struck me as funny and somewhat pathetic that I was having a conversation about suicide and that this man, who had called the police because he was going to kill himself, was asking advice on how to kill himself. Funny because he was asking the wrong guy, I was clearly unsuccessful.

After a while I began to sit at the same table with the same people and manage a conversation or two. Usually about what drugs we were on, some past experiences, complaints or advice about the food and small talk. Strangely, I began to look up to a guy named Adam. He was in for drugs and alcohol for the second time. He was articulate, smart, funny and he knew the ropes. He also was trying to get better and get a job and hopefully get out. He was at the time rooming with the vilest human being I have ever met. His roommate smelled like vomit, shit, and rot. He left a waft of stench everywhere he went and you could smell him as soon as he entered the room and for minutes after. He also refused to shower. I saw an opportunity to maybe get a room with Adam because room mates were scary and unpredictable.

You never knew when your roommate was going to leave and you sure as hell didn't know who and what would replace them. Patients came and went. One kid came in and was so sedated that he drooled uncontrollably.

Other patients came in and had the look of junkies on the edge of madness and violence. My roommate was not so good, he snored horribly, he never bathed, he brought food into the room (something he was not supposed to do) and left half eaten things and garbage lying around. He spilled things in the room, he grunted and moaned a lot, and he stayed in our room all day and night. After Adam's stinky roommate was finally sent somewhere else, I suggested to Adam that we should room together.

We had kind of become almost friends and I wanted to avoid for the moment at least getting a horrible roommate if my roommate were to leave. Adam also did not want to get another nasty roommate, and he claimed not to snore, which was good news for my sleep. (As I found out later, he did snore, but not as bad as my former roommate.) We convinced the nurses to move me, and my situation improved a little, at least for the moment. My former roommate was a little offended and I possibly hurt his feelings, but I had to look out for my better interest.

As I entered what I think was my third or fourth week in this hell I began to consider ECT (Electro- convulsive Therapy) treatment. As I said before, my mother had had something similar and cruder, but it worked for her, so why not me? I suggested the possibility of this to the evil doctor on one of our infrequent visits and he referred me to the doctor with the limp, as he was an expert in this procedure. Eventually it came to pass, and I went in for my first treatment.

Electroconvulsive Therapy is a procedure done under anesthesia in which small electric currents pass through the brain, intentionally causing a brief seizure. ECT seems to change brain chemistry, and these changes can quickly change symptoms of some mental health disorders. You've probably seen a crude version of it in movies where it's used to torture prisoners to get information out of them. This fortunately is not as severe or as long. The day came for my first ECT.

Before this procedure I was given an IV and set up monitors. I was also asked a certain number of questions before and after the treatment to see how greatly my memory was affected. For the first few treatments I was given this horrible drug that prevents you from producing saliva. This was to supposedly prevent me from choking. I hated this drug as it left me completely dried out for hours after the treatment. It also caused me to have a sore throat, and I couldn't eat without severe throat pain. After my third treatment my throat became raw and I had trouble swallowing. This never went away from the remainder of my stay, and I was diagnosed with strep throat after I was discharged. I requested that this medication not be given anymore and thankfully the anesthesiologist was okay with it. Going under anesthesia is awful.

I still remember the distinct smell of the anesthetic entering the facemask. It is scary to lose complete consciousness, to lose time, to become nothing and remember nothing. I remember trying my hardest to stay conscious, paying attention to the clock on the wall and noting the time, holding one finger out to somehow not lose complete consciousness. Of course, it never worked. I would lose five minutes of my life three times a week. After the procedure I was very tired, but I did not want to sleep in my room during the day because this would look bad for me getting out.

I continued to play the game, getting out of bed in the morning, going to group therapy, not asking for drugs during the day, and receiving ECT treatments. Eventually this led to a meeting with the evil doctor and my wife to get out. I would agree to continue the ECT treatments out-patient and schedule appointments with a therapist and psychiatrist. I would finally get out of this hell.

By the time I was discharged, I did not feel suicidal and I did not have crippling anxiety, nor did I feel depressed. I felt numb. That's the best way that I can describe it, just numb. I cannot pinpoint or describe the moment that my anxiety and depression subsided; it just came to be. Perhaps the relief and joy of finally getting out of that horrible place changed me, allowed me to feel a little hope. Maybe the inpatient ECT treatments worked to some degree and reset my brain that part that provides that essential human belief for survival, that belief that somehow, some way, things would be alright.

I felt a determination to never go backwards, to never let myself get as bad as when I felt hopeless. To never feel…. that way again. I had not only survived an attempt at my own life, but I had made it through the confinement in that hell of a space generously called a mental rehabilitation hospital. There was no rehabilitation to be found there. It was a holding place to house the unwanted and outcasts of society. It was for me, a place that tried to break me, to kill me, a place where hope dies. Ironically, it was much like the public school system I knew too well. Understaffed, out of touch, lacking resources, and a shortage of qualified staff. A staff that had been beaten down by the hopelessness of the institution and the system. A staff that had grown callous, almost resentful of the very people they were trying to help. A staff that was just trying to survive another shift.

It's not like I was completely cured when I was released, I still had some anxiety and did not go out of the house for some weeks to come. I felt fragile and frail. I had lost a lot of weight. I was extremely tired. The weeks of little to no sleep I suffered in the hospital took its toll. My life became going in early in the mornings for more ECT treatments, sitting on the couch and watching TV, doing some chores around the house and sleeping.

Eventually I stopped ECT treatments. I think I had twelve treatments in all and that was enough for me, I wanted to stop. My wife reluctantly agreed and I began the long, slow process of trying to make sense of my life post suicide attempt.

Guilt was my biggest hurdle, guilt has always been a problem for me, useless, pointless guilt. I was filled with it. Somehow, I had to find a way to forgive myself and accept the forgiveness of others. This would not be easy. This would take a long time. The one thing that I was most sure of and felt most strongly about was that I could never ever hurt my family again. I was resolved to get better; I had to get better. I would do whatever it took to get better. But how, how would I ever explain what happened to me? How could I explain why I tried to take my life? How could I explain the unexplainable? Did I even need to attempt to explain any of it?

Of course, I could never guarantee that I would not get sick again. That was something that could never be possible. Let's just say that my wife did not feel 100% sure that I would not try to take my life again, and who could blame her. She had endured her own hell as only the spouse of someone who tries to kill themselves could. I had ultimately betrayed her.

I had destroyed the trust that we had together. I had performed the most selfish act possible. Suicide! There I said it. Suicide, suicide, suicide! It's such a horrible all-encompassing word. It has a finality, a visual association. Yet it conjures up a feeling of emptiness, a terrible void. When you have experienced it first or second hand it becomes a very powerful word, a word that should not be spoken lightly or heard without thought. It's strange how non-members of the suicide club can throw that word around freely, sometimes jokingly. I was guilty of using that word with a nonchalant casual attitude, as if I knew what it meant and the power that it had. Now, every time I hear the word I cringe, as if hit with a blow to the heart, a body punch, a piercing stab. I cower like a dog when I hear that word.

We can think of the ways in which people commit suicide, like hanging oneself, blowing one's head off, sitting in the car in the garage with engine running, swallowing pills or even jumping off a bridge or a building. What we don't think about or talk much about is the person who finds us. The person to first see their loved one in a repugnant and often horrifying and gruesome condition. These images are often burned into their memory for a very long time. They are the ones that must live and make sense out of a senseless brutal act, often dealing with a huge swing of emotions from trauma, guilt, anxiety and anger. My son may have been the first to find me, but he thought I was only sleeping and did not want to wake me up. My wife, knowing my condition, instantly knew something was wrong. She rushed home and called 911 when she discovered I was unresponsive.

Would she ever forgive me? Could she ever trust me again? How had she survived the last unknown number of weeks of my incarceration? She did not trust me. She locked up all the medications in the house at first. She called me regularly throughout the day to check on me. I had broken her trust, and it would take a while to earn it back.

I accepted her mistrust; it would take time. In the meantime, I hugged my son and wife frequently. I went to the doctor about my shoulder and sore throat and eventually they both got better. I attended my son's high school tennis matches. I began to play tennis again. Gradually I began to leave the house occasionally seeing friends, but not without an acute awareness of what they might be thinking about me.

I was also very worried about what my son was experiencing with his friends and how he was dealing with my failures. I asked him if he had any questions about anything, you know like, "Why did you do it?" "What was wrong with you?" "Are you better now?" but he would simply say "I'm just glad you're better." He made it easy for me, he accepted me, his love never wavered. It was simple for him, "you're here, that's all I care about." I did not have to explain anything to him, at least not yet.

I am medicated and it bothers me to be so dependent, but I take my medicine religiously. Being around friends is still hard, I can't help thinking they know what I had done and that they might be judging me. They all seem to give me unusually long hugs. Guilt and shame are my constant companions, but this has lessened a little over time. I see a therapist regularly who helps me and I see a psychiatrist that seems to care about my health and me. It is hard for me to maintain eye contact. It is hard to see close friends, and it is hard not to be reminded of the way I was and my attempted suicide. I am reminded every time I walk into our bedroom; I am reminded when I drive by the hospital or hear a siren.

I am reminded every time I drive by the grocery store, I once worked at and cannot bring myself back in to. I worry about those horrible feelings of hopelessness and fear returning. I worry about the future, I worry about my children and wife, I worry about money, I worry, but not hopelessly with crippling fear, but now, with responsibility and with the frail and fragile belief that everyone clings to. It will be alright. Somehow it will be alright. Somehow it will turn out just the way it was supposed to. Which is to say with utmost ambiguity and randomness, it will be what it is.

Of the greatest things that have happened to me since I was released from the hospital was watching my son play his last high school tennis match. He was sad about it all coming to an end and very emotional. He came up to me and hugged me tight.

Crying he said simply and repeatedly, "I'm so glad you're here." Not there, there in some horrible, unthinkable tragic memory, but here in the present with you my son, and my wife and daughter and sisters and family and friends. "Here" where I have suffered mental illnesses handed down from my mother and father and from their mothers and fathers before them. "Here," surviving a suicide attempt and the shame and guilt that comes with it. "Here" in the final chapters of a life of someone who thinks way too much. "Here" in the fragile existence of someone who has been to hell and has clawed his way back to the now. Finally, "here," in the narrow-medicated space between mania and depression, always knowing that "it" could return and that I am never, ever completely safe. This knowing does not weigh on me like it used to, it does not cripple me, it does not keep me from living, it is there, a suppressed part of me, a gene passed down, a propensity I must at all cost control.

In the end, I am grateful. I was lucky. I was blessed. I am not an overly religious man, but sometimes I chalk things up to just being blessed. Whatever you want to call it, I have been given a gift, the greatest gift one could ever receive. It is the gift of a second chance, "a new life please." Ironically my song. With the risk of sounding corny and being a cliché, I have found a deep appreciation for being alive. I have a sense of gratefulness that still to this day remains.

I say this with the utmost humility, but, it is somewhat empowering to have survived a suicide attempt. Nothing really upsets me too much. I shake adversity off fairly easily. I don't mind things going wrong sometimes. I don't worry too much about money. It is simply not worth it for me to worry. I've had a lifetime full of worry, enough is enough! I mean I have been to the lowest of low places. (It feels risky saying such things,) For these reasons, I find it necessary to check in with my wife and doctors regularly at the risk of being manic. I guess it's okay to be hopeful. How do I explain that everything from this point on is just extra, gravy, a bonus? Of course, I say this with the great caution, and wary that when life feels too good there's something waiting in the shadows, something awful and tragic.

There is so much to lose, and it can be taken away just like that. (I snap my fingers here.) For now, I'm going to ride it. What else can I do? Here goes nothing.

As the days grew closer to Patrick's memorial I grew more and more anxious. I wasn't sure I would be able to muster up the strength to go. I wasn't sure I could stand the scrutiny real, or imagined. I didn't make up my mind until the day finally came, I would go, I would be brave, I would be strong, for my family. Patrick committed suicide. He was successful. He hung himself in the basement after the Paul McCartney concert we both went to. (separately) I often ask myself, "why after the Paul McCartney concert?" "Why then?" His suicide sucked the breath out of me. It floored me and brought back feelings I've tried to stay away from for a year and a half now. He left behind a wife and two young children. It was the ultimate tragedy. I didn't want to go to his memorial because that could have very, very well been me. It should have been me. If I had been successful and Patrick had attended my funeral, maybe he wouldn't have killed himself. Maybe....

I knew that by attending I was going to have to face the hard truth in front of my wife's family, who I'm sure knew about my attempt at suicide a year ago April. I knew that this memorial was going to bring up questions in the minds of family and friends and more importantly, my wife and son. The memorial took place at the school where Patrick taught. There was a large turnout of students, faculty, friends and family. Several people attempted to speak. His children spoke and broke down grotesquely. I looked over at my son and saw the tears silently falling down his cheeks and I lost it. I grabbed him and held him tight to me and I said repeatedly, "I'm so sorry, I'm so sorry." He comforted me, of all things, he comforted me and said very simply, "It's okay, I'm so glad you're here." He sobbed, and I repeated and sobbed, "I'm sorry, I'm sorry" We held onto each other, clinging together in that moment of ultimate realization of what I had done to my son, and my family. In between the sobbing I said, "we're okay, we're okay," I couldn't tell you how long we clung to each other and sobbed. I felt the shame, the guilt, and the ultimate humiliation in front of my friends and family. (And strangers alike.)

The consequences of what I had tried to do laid out bare, with bones and muscle and cartilage, and sinews of fat dripping off the carcass of my selfish act. It was my confession and my penance all in one, shared with family and friends but most importantly with my son and wife. We were lucky, blessed even, we still had each other. I had failed where Patrick had succeeded. It should have been me; it could have been me. We felt the terrible empty tragedy and sorrow of Patrick's wife and children.

The bitter sad irony was not lost on us. Were there signs Patrick was depressed? Had Patrick been under care by a therapist or doctor? Had he been thinking of this for a while or was it a desperate moment, a split-second decision that will last a lifetime? There are no answers for this act of desperation, only questions. I understand that desperation, that moment, and now those tragic consequences. Our family will celebrate each year, we will celebrate Patrick's life on St. Patrick's Day with a toast of one of his favorite beverages, Irish Whiskey. We did so just the other night. My wife, my son, and I. Cheers Patrick, cheers to you!

In his later years, my father would often quote Dylan Thomas' famous poem, "do not go gentle into that good night" as a reminder to himself to not give up, and to find purpose and new experiences in his later years. Fight to the death if you will. It is a quote that has stuck with me like many other things my father said. I am fully retired now and trying to enjoy it without guilt. I still miss serving people, doing something of consequence to do some good in this messed up world. I'm an assistant coach for the boys and girls high school tennis teams so that helps a little. I do feel a bit muted and sometimes drugged, but I'm okay with that because I know what the alternative is and I am resolved never to go back.

I can find moments of contentedness and relish time with my wife and children. I'm alive! I live with cautious optimism, knowing that I am never ever truly safe from the anxiety and depression that once took me to the edge. But I do not live in fear anymore, and I do not live only in the future. I live in the now. Fuck fear! Fuck the future! In the immortal words of Doris Day, I sing to anxiety and I sing to depression, I sing to ambiguity and finally I sing to the randomness of life, "Que Sera, Sera" mother fucker. "Que Sera, Sera!

Thank you for reading Random Ambiguity. Sharing these deeply personal thoughts and experiences with the world was not easy, and I am incredibly grateful you chose to share them with me. If my story resonated with you, moved you, or made you think, please consider leaving an honest review. Your feedback helps other readers discover this book. If you know someone who is struggling with mental health or you yourself are struggling, please don't suffer alone. Get help, talk to someone, keep searching for a therapist that is right for you and who genuinely cares about your health. They are out there. If you are in immediate need of help, call 988 suicide and crisis line

About the Author

Joel Sissel obviously thinks way too much for his own good. He is for sure an observer, a lover of history, a perpetual student of life and the author of *Random Ambiguity.* Born in 1960 in a suburb of Philadelphia, he has lived in Maryland, Florida, and North Carolina, but was eventually captured by Iowans and held captive there for most of his adult life. He was a middle school teacher for over 20 years. Before that he was a guitarist, singer and songwriter in many bands including 23 Lies. He later went on to write, produce and record his own music under the band name Psychedelic Doo Doo. The songs referenced in his book including; "A New Life Please, I Can't Let Go, Sex and Love, and Sister Desire" can be heard on the music platform Bandcamp. When not writing, Joel can be found on the tennis court, in the garden, or travelling. He currently lives in Des Moines, Iowa with his wife and son.